I0148641

RICH TOWARD GOD

Doing Life and Business God's Way

MARK NOBLIN

Published by
The Rock Outreach, Inc.

www.RichTowardGod.org

Copyright © 2008 by The Rock Outreach, Inc.

No part of this publication may be reproduced, stored in a retrieval system, or transmitted in any form or by any means -- electronic, mechanical, photocopying, recording, scanning or otherwise -- except as permitted under Sections 107 of 108 of the 1976 United States Copyright Act, without the prior written permission of the Publisher.
All Scripture quotations, unless otherwise indicated, are taken from the Holy Bible New international Version ® NIV ®. Copyright © 1973, 1978, 1984 by International Bible Society. Used by permission of Zondervan Publishing House. All rights reserved.

Cover design by D Group, Dallas, Texas.

Contents

This book is dedicated to all those who resolve to seek first His Kingdom and His righteousness, and to the One who strengthens us to do so.

x

Acknowledgements

Special thanks to my wife Margaret who has been encouraging me for years to write this book. She is a great sounding board and wrote all the study questions as well. Next to Jesus, she is God's greatest gift to me.

Also gratitude for the support from the other members of the board of The Rock Outreach, Inc. -- Dan Vick, Yvonne Valasek, Colin McGraw, Bill Wendl and my wife Margaret . We stand together in a vision to make a difference for the Kingdom at home and in Africa, a very challenging part of the world.

I continue to be encouraged by the fruit shown by the children, university students and adults in The Rock family in Africa as they apply the truths in this book from God's Word to their lives. Without them and the faithful supporters of this ministry, this book would not be possible.

Preface

This is a book written for those who have embraced Jesus as their sole means of salvation and who believe the Bible is the inerrant Word of God.

Others can benefit from the principles in the book, but ultimately without faith in God the Father, Son and Holy Spirit as revealed in the Bible they will find no satisfactory solutions.

The book is meant to be a discipleship and exhortation tool for believers. It is not written to be politically correct nor sensitive to cultural mores which go against God's teaching.

In early critiques of the book, one professional Christian writer questioned the "tone" of the book. Although my most important critic, my wife Margaret, had not addressed the tone earlier, the other critique caused her to question whether the writing was too harsh.

I explained to her on a Saturday morning over breakfast at Bubba's, one of our favorite family diners, that I was writing the book as a coach, not a counselor.

"It's like a halftime talk for a football coach in a game where his team is not performing to potential," I said. "The coach doesn't gently sit the team down and say, 'Now, boys, you need to remember what you learned during practice. I don't want to hurt your feelings but you are not doing as well on your assignments as you might.'"

No, the coach would more likely say, "We are getting our brains beat out. Execute. Execute. Execute. Do your job individually and as a team and get after it with all you've got. We can win this thing!"

That's me – the coach. The coach's desire is to strain the maximum potential out of his players and to win.

The football analogy reminds me of a book written by a friend of mine. *The Utlimate Business Playbook*[1] by Mike Grayson is a framework for getting everyone involved in an endeavor on the same playbook. Each player must know their responsibilities for each play. The next level is understanding others' assignments for each play. They must work together with a common vision for the same goal – scoring a touchdown.

As believers, the Bible is our playbook and this book is designed to help you learn how to execute your plays.

For purposes of this book, if you have surrendered to Jesus for your salvation, you already have won the game. You have become a part of a team which is called the Body of Christ, the gathering of all saints (those redeemed by Jesus).

What this book addresses is, "What role do you want to play on that team?" Professional football players can receive a Super Bowl ring just by sitting on the bench of a winning team. People can go to heaven by sitting on the sidelines after salvation. But wouldn't you rather be glorifying God on the playing field rather than just sitting on the bench?

Sometimes players come off the bench to become stars. The bench is not your destiny. Satan tries to tell us we are not good enough to get off the bench and in the game because of our past transgressions. That is a lie! God does not care about who we have been, He cares about who we are. When I speak in this book of things like divorce or "white" lies it is not my intent to judge anyone and make them feel doomed to the bench. To the contrary, the goal is to encourage them to claim God's truth, be healed from their injuries and get in the game, and also to help others to avoid the same mistakes that keep some on the bench.

And then there are those like me, who sometimes just need a wake up call. As I relate in the book, God allowed severe consequences upon me before He got my attention.

I also remember when I played defensive tackle on the Highland Park High School football team in the late '60s. In case you haven't heard, high school football is a really big deal in Texas. Our team would practice long and hard for games. The coaches would review the previous game films of every opponent and give very specific assignments to each player for the game.

For instance, I was told if a guard pulls this way, then I should react in a certain way. Or, if the offensive line sets up for pass blocking, I would

1   Grayson, Mike. *The Ultimate Business Playbook*. MGM Adventures, Ltd., 2008

react another way. Even though these assignments were drilled into my head, I realized after a couple of games that, after the whistle blew and the ball was kicked off, I ignored everything I had been taught and just chased after the ball.

When I finally realized I was not following the playbook the coaches gave me and began to follow their lead, my play improved radically. Soon I was making more tackles and before I knew it, the offenses were not running at me nearly as often.

The bottom line is: When in doubt, follow the directions (or playbook). This book is designed to help you follow the only divinely inspired playbook – the Bible.

Now go win one for the home team!

Introduction
Rich Toward God

First off, let me shoot straight. If you are looking for a list of ways to get into God's favor so you can prosper financially, read no farther.

If, on the other hand, your desire is to be rich toward God, (Luke 12:21) read on. The Bible tells us if we gain the whole world but lose our soul, we gain nothing (Matthew 16:26). I like the saying that we can't take our worldly things with us when we die, but we can send them on ahead.

Jesus said it this way: "Do not store up for yourselves treasures on earth, where moth and rust destroy, and where thieves break in and steal. But store up for yourselves treasures in heaven, where moth and rust do not destroy, and where thieves do not break in and steal. For where your treasure is, there your heart will be also" (Matthew 6:19-21).

Where is your heart? Where is your treasure? What are your priorities? If your heart is in your personal significance and your trust is in your possessions, you need to read on. If your treasure is only what is in your business, career, portfolio or property, you are allowing yourself to be robbed of God's purpose in your life. Many Christians convince themselves their trust is in the Lord, but the evidence of where and how they invest their lives and the conspicuous display of their earthly treasures betrays them.

The rich young ruler (Matthew 19:16-23) was such a man. When he asked how he could gain eternal life, Jesus told him to follow all the commandments. The young man (notice we are never even told his name) said he had done so, but even he knew he was still lacking. Jesus looked straight through him and advised him to go sell all his possessions and give them to the poor.

"When the young man heard this, he went away sad," the Bible says, "because he had great wealth." He thought he loved the Lord, but in truth he loved his possessions even more. The lesson here is not that Jesus calls everyone to give everything away, but rather that He calls us to be prepared to do so because our allegiance to Him should make our worldly possessions seem irrelevant.

What Has You?

It's been said that it's not what you have, it's what has you. Let's be honest here. This is tough teaching. Jesus' disciples, hearing the dialogue between Him and the rich young man, asked, "Who then can be saved?"

A highly successful and godly businessman who invited me under his wing when I was a new believer surprised me on a summer walk one evening by confiding, "Mark, I just don't know if I could do that. I just don't think I could give up everything." My friend and mentor knows the pull of the world and, in fact, what he said is true, as evidenced by Jesus' response to the disciples' question of who can be saved.

"With man this is impossible, but with God all things are possible," Jesus said. So if you are trying to balance your business and possessions with your relationship with the Lord on your own terms, you might as well give up. Instead, follow the manual (God's Word).

Jesus has been very clear in setting our priorities for us: "'Love the Lord your God with all your heart and with all your soul and with all your mind.' This is the first and greatest commandment. And the second is like it: 'Love your neighbor as yourself.' All the Law and the Prophets hang on these two commandments" (Matthew 22:37-40).

Our Lord also is precise on how we accomplish the greatest commandment of loving Him: "If you love me, you will obey what I command" (John 14:15).

If we are to show our love by obeying, we need to know His standards as laid out in the Bible! That is the purpose of this book. First, we will examine the condition of your heart. As a professed follower of Jesus, are you really, through your actions and energies, who you claim to be? If not, how can you become that person? God has given us very clear instructions in His Word on how we are to conduct ourselves in all aspects of our life, including business and career. We will examine the characteristics of a godly business person as presented in the Bible. And we will see how God would have us lead others by example to honor Him.

Persecution Guaranteed

The virtues God desires from us often go against our ideas of business as usual. When practiced, they undoubtedly will produce persecution from a fallen, compromised world that seeks to justify itself against the righteous behavior we are to exhibit in obedience to the Lord. We are called to be God pleasers, not people pleasers, (James 4:4) which goes against our human nature.

I remember several years ago being like Peter when he denied Jesus. I was in a bar with a group of corporate sales people. I was being a good Baptist by drinking seltzer water and lime as jokes were being told. One young woman spoke up, "No one here is a strong Christian, are they?" I had a few seconds to declare myself but didn't. The woman went on to tell a blasphemous joke. Afraid of being persecuted in the business world for my faith, I had turned away from my Savior for just a split second.

God has forgiven me, but I must confess I'm still struggling to forgive myself for that incident. I was afraid of persecution but since have prayed never to fall short in standing for the Lord again.

I remember a few years later having lunch with a decision maker at a large corporate account for which I served as the sales team manager. The discussion of evolution came up and there were derogatory remarks about creationism. When I expressed my belief in the biblical account of creation, my relationship with the customer, and the account, took a definite downward spiral.

But the damage done to that relationship, and the resulting economic hardship it caused, paled to the sadness I had experienced earlier when I failed to stand for the Lord.

I also left another corporate job because I was being urged by my boss to falsify orders. The boss did not really want to cheat and steal, but his rationale was that because all of my peers under other managers were doing it, it was making his sales numbers look bad by comparison.

A Bull's-eye for the Evil One

When we are living a life pleasing to God, particularly in the marketplace, we must expect also to be a target of Satan. We will discuss who the enemy really is, how to recognize when the battle is engaged, and how to emerge victoriously, giving glory to God.

Here is a tip: Keeping your guard up for Satan does not mean looking out for a guy with horns and a pitchfork. (That image is a trick of the enemy so we won't take him seriously) No, be on the lookout for such things as broken relationships stemming from miscommunication and temptations being put in your path. Satan is the father of lies (John 8:44) and the master of confusion. Beware of beguilement, jealousy, envy, greed, lust.

Whenever God is getting ready to move our ministry to a new level, my wife Margaret and I have learned to anticipate the attempt by the enemy to stop us in our tracks.

He attacks by having us misunderstand one another or ascribe incorrect motives to each other's words or actions. We can become divided until we realize what is happening. We call upon the Lord to defeat the enemy's attempts to turn us against ourselves and we can then move forward.

Some people as they succeed in business begin to believe the adulation they receive. The headiness of power can lead to pride, perhaps Satan's biggest weapon against us.

A "successful" pastor who God had used in amazing ways to impact thousands of lives once told me, "You know, Mark, I could have been a very successful businessman." The pastor was confused, thinking he was responsible for all the funds raised for his ministry and the churches, schools and clinics built. Pride overtook him as he gave glory to himself rather than God. After all, pride is the original sin.

Who Really Is In Control?

Closely related to pride is our desire to be in control. We are called to do everything as if unto the Lord, not man (Colossians 3:23). That means we give our best to honor Him while realizing our limitations and dependence upon Him. Frequently, I fall into the trap of trying too hard and depending on my own wisdom and strength to accomplish a task instead of turning to the Lord. The result is frustration, anxiety and an inflated sense of self.

The Book of James gives us a reality check. "Now listen, you who say, 'Today or tomorrow we will go to this or that city, spend a year there, carry on business and make money.'"   Why, you do not even know what will happen tomorrow. What is your life? You are a mist that appears for a little while and then vanishes. Instead, you ought to say, "If it is the Lord's will, we will live and do this or that." As it is, you boast and brag. All such boasting is evil" (James 4:13-16).

Satan also comes at us with opportunities to stumble sexually and financially – or both – as I have seen tragically in more cases than I wish to remember. Yes, believers can "buy the lie" of Satan with devastating repercussions. And, the moment you think you are immune, you are the most vulnerable.

The Bankrupt "Prosperity Gospel"

Returning to the original point of checklists for financial prosperity, I will state for the record I believe the current "Prosperity Gospel" being taught today is a distortion of God's Word. The principle that when we sow into God's Kingdom financially, that He will provide an abundant harvest for us to reap is correct to a point. But, always our heart and motives trump our methods to gain God's favor. God's challenge in Malachi to test Him in giving and He will "throw open the floodgates of heaven and pour out so much blessing that you will not have room enough for it" (Malachi 3:10) is preceded by His command, "return to me, and I will return to you" (Malachi 3:7). Returning to Him does not mean sending a check; it means demonstrating love and obedience to His Word: "Ever since the time of your forefathers you have turned away from my decrees and have not kept them" (Malachi 3:7).

Some people want to relegate God to being some type of cosmic Coke machine. You put the money in and out pops your soda. But if the soda doesn't appear, you grumble and kick and shake the machine. We can't buy God off and He is onto our impure motives.

"To obey is better than sacrifice, and to heed is better than the fat of rams" (1 Samuel 15:22).

"You do not delight in sacrifice, or I would bring it; you do not take pleasure in burnt offerings. The sacrifices of God are a broken spirit; a broken and contrite heart, O God, you will not despise" (Psalms 51:16-17).

Indeed, God tells us He hates our offerings when they are for the wrong motives (Amos 5:21). In contrast, God loves a cheerful giver who does not give reluctantly or under compulsion (2 Corinthians 9:7). In other words, He loves us and our hearts purified by Jesus more than anything else.

We tend to view God's blessings from a material perspective. If we give money or strive to follow His teachings, we want Him to bless us back with money. Often, God's blessings are not monetary. Our greatest blessing from Him is the fellowship we enjoy as a result of being His obedient children. When we follow the greatest commandment, everything we do for Him is out of love and it is blessing enough for us to demonstrate that love to our Maker. Anything else, including financial gain, is gravy!

Of course, the Bible does teach sound, practical financial principles and concepts that will help anyone who applies them manage their business and finances more effectively. Still, there is no guarantee of business or financial prosperity, even though the Lord does promise to provide for those who serve Him (Psalm 37:25).

And the wicked do prosper financially on this earth (Jeremiah 12:1), apparently unaware of what awaits them in eternity. God is sovereign and His ways are not our ways (Isaiah 55:8-9). He blesses as He chooses. Consider Joseph, son of Jacob. He led a righteous life, overcoming rejection by his brothers who sold him into slavery, false sexual accusations against him and imprisonment. God blessed Joseph's fidelity and righteousness. He became the second most powerful man in all of Egypt.

Solomon is another interesting case. When God offered him "whatever you want me to give you" in a dream (1 Kings 3:5) he asked for "a discerning heart to govern your people" (1 Kings 3:9) rather than riches. As a result, God not only provided him with the wisdom he requested, but also riches and honor "so that in your lifetime you will have no equal among kings" (1 Kings 3:13).

Solomon, however, allowed his possessions and power to become a curse to him as he took on "seven hundred wives of royal birth and three hundred concubines, and his wives led him astray" (1 Kings 11:3) by turning him to other gods.

Money Never Satisfies

"Whoever loves money never has money enough;" Solomon concludes, "whoever loves wealth is never satisfied with his income. This too is meaningless" (Ecclesiastes 5:10).

It took Solomon his whole life to learn these words the Lord has shared with us in the Bible: "Now all has been heard; here is the conclusion of the matter: Fear God and keep his commandments, for this is the whole duty of man" (Ecclesiastes 12:13). That is your whole duty as a Christian business person.

Others who feared God were blessed in ways we cannot understand. Of the 11 disciples remaining after Judas' betrayal, only four died natural deaths. Four were crucified, one was stoned, one was speared and one was beheaded. The Bible tells us the martyrs have a special place in heaven (Revelation 6:9). And Stephen, as he was stoned for standing for righteousness, was given an amazing glimpse of heaven and saw "Jesus standing at the right hand of God" (Acts 7:55). Elsewhere in the Bible, Jesus sits at the right hand of God, but here He was standing in honor of Stephen's faithfulness!

It is shameful how misguided people induce others to give to the Lord or obey Him in expectation of immediate financial or tangible return. We see this in the U.S., but it also has infected other parts of the world, particularly Africa. People are promised healing, jobs, spouses, children, prosperity or whatever they can dream up if they will just put enough money in the collection plate. This is defaming to the name of God and the leaders who are engaging in this practice will be held accountable on Judgment Day (Revelation 20:11-15). I don't think it will be pretty.

A Conduit for the Lord

So what does all this have to do with "Doing Business God's Way"? If you want to please Him in your work or business, you need to start by examining why you are doing what you are doing in your personal and business life. What is the condition of your heart? What is the cure, if needed? This book will help you find out and then point to Biblical truths of how you can please, honor and glorify God by doing business His way, overcoming the world and the enemy's schemes in the Lord's power.

If you surrender to the Lord and His Word, He will be faithful to bless you according to His plan for your life. And, as you are blessed, you will have a wonderful opportunity in your career or business to be used by Him. God's message is that as He blesses us, He will use us to bless others as well.

This was his message to Abraham:

"I will make you into a great nation
and I will bless you;
I will make your name great,
and you will be a blessing.
I will bless those who bless you,
and whoever curses you I will curse;
and all peoples on earth
will be blessed through you." (Genesis 12:2-3)

This is Doing Business God's Way: Loving Him and obeying Him so you can be an instrument to receive and pass on His blessings.

Introduction

Discussion Questions

1. What two principles in life guide your decisions? What is the duty of Man?

2. What does the culture tell us about what is important versus what the Bible says?

3. Explain what the Bible says will bring peace.

4. How do expectations in life that are influenced by culture impact the "condition of the heart?" How does God expect us to show love?

5. What influence do these expectations have in our families and relationships?

Personal Reflections

1. What is in my heart? What thoughts are on my mind most during the day?

2. How often do I consider what God thinks about my decisions? Do I believe God sees my motives?

3. Examine the evidence. What do my actions and the way I spend my time say about what I treasure?

4. What would my children or other family members say if they were asked what I value the most?

5. Where is my heart? Where is my treasure/? What are my priorities? What has me?

Chapter 1
What is the Condition of Your Heart?

Time for a Checkup

In many ways, the condition of our spiritual heart can be compared to our vital and irreplaceable organ that pumps blood throughout our body.

If you went in for a medical checkup, your doctor might check your cholesterol levels to determine if your arteries are in danger of being clogged. Perhaps you would have a stress test to gauge your heart. If there were warning signs, he might do an angiogram to provide images of the blood flow through the major arteries. If the blood flow was restricted, he might do angioplasty (like a Roto-Rooter for the heart) to clean you out. Or maybe put in a stint to keep the passage clear. Or even open up your chest and do bypass surgery to take slices of healthy arteries from your leg and use them to replace and re-route them in your heart.

The checkup for our spiritual heart is similar. Cholesterol does not build up overnight in our veins and arteries, but slowly over a period of many years. Many of us suffer from spiritual cholesterol leading to impure motives. Over time, unhealthy habits like greed, envy, lust, pride, vanity, and anger begin to develop plaque which blocks our spiritual veins and arteries. We're not talking here about physically stealing, committing adultery or committing violence against someone. We're talking about wandering minds that give the devil a foothold. When I sold computers, there was an old acronym, GIGO (garbage in, garbage out). When we expose ourselves to worldly influences, the "plaque" begins to build up in our spiritual veins. And Jesus, always one to raise the bar in His teaching, tells us that spiritually the thinking equates to the doing (Matthew 5:21, 28).

Another cause of heart problems is lack of exercise. We are told to do "cardio" exercises to get our heart rate up. Inactivity can lead to problems. Spiritually, it is the same. Our spiritual cardio exercises are spending regular time in the Bible, praying, fellowshipping with other believers, worshipping and attending church. The cardio helps head off the creeping bad habits. Sometimes God uses a stress test to reveal the condition of our hearts. When we are lulled to sleep in our routine and fall into bad practices, He presents a crisis in our lives to wake us up and become dependent on Him again. Sometimes the process is tough (like angioplasty or stints) but it doesn't split us open.

When that doesn't work, He allows us to suffer great pain inflicted by our own behavior (this is like open heart surgery). He uses our own sin to rough us up and get our attention. Then He loves us enough to forgive and bring us back to Him.

One of the keys for the healthy condition of our heart is a good diet. "Finally, brothers, whatever is true, whatever is noble, whatever is right, whatever is pure, whatever is lovely, whatever is admirable – if anything is excellent or praiseworthy – think about such things. Whatever you have learned or received or heard from me, or seen in me – put it into practice. And the God of peace will be with you" (Philippians 4:8-9).

Spiritual discipline is another key: prayer, Bible study, church.

So, how is the condition of your heart? Where can you go for a checkup? The Bible is the place.

There is some bad news (the good news comes later). "The heart is deceitful above all things and beyond cure. Who can understand it?" (Jeremiah 17:9).

In the Beginning

We don't have to go any farther than Adam and Eve to see the problems emerge in the human heart. Adam and Eve succumbed to the devil's lies and disobeyed God by tasting of the tree of good and evil. Disobedience and the desire to be like God overcame them and corrupted the hearts of all mankind to come.

Their "heart failure" and God's plan to restore man's right relationship with Him comprises the whole story of the Bible from beginning to end and is the reason the perfect Son of God had to come from heaven to earth to die on a cross as the perfect sacrifice and satisfaction to God for all who believe.

Next came Cain and Abel, the sons of Adam and Eve. Abel kept flocks and Cain worked the soil. In time, Cain brought some of the fruits of the soil to sacrifice to the Lord and Abel brought fat portions from some of the first born of his flocks. God looked with favor on Abel's sacrifice, but not so with Cain's.

"Then the Lord said to Cain, 'Why are you angry? Why is your face downcast? If you do what is right, will you not be accepted? But if you do not do what is right, sin is crouching at your door; it desires to have you, but you must master it'" (Genesis 4:6-7).

It is interesting to note that the Scriptures do not specifically tell us why Cain's sacrifice was not favored by God. Why do you think God favored Abel's offering over Cain? I believe the only logical conclusion is that Cain's sacrifice, unlike Abel's, was not offered with a pure heart. Perhaps he did so begrudgingly, or with a sense of obligation. Note God admonished him: "If you do what is right, will you not be accepted?"

But instead of listening to God, sin overcame an angry Cain who ended up jealously murdering his own brother.

What does this Scripture say to you in your business or career? It tells you to examine your heart and motives. Are you honoring and glorifying God in your work or are you only giving Him lip service and going through the motions in an attempt to satisfy Him? Is your motive to enrich yourself or to be rich toward God? "A faithful man will be richly blessed, but one eager to get rich will not go unpunished" (Proverbs 28:20).

Taking Control

The first king of Israel is another study in heart failure. Saul began with great promise. He was an "impressive young man without equal among the Israelites" (1 Samuel 9:2). God had picked him out in acceding to the Israelites' demand for a king.

But Saul's heart was turned inward: He trusted his own intellect and instincts more than God's commands and wisdom.

He was told directly by God's prophet, Samuel, to travel to Gilgal and wait seven days before going to battle with the Philistines. On the seventh day, Saul became impatient for Samuel to appear. The enemy was gathering against him and his troops were fearful and began to scatter.

Taking matters into his own hands, Saul himself offered a sacrifice to God, only to see Samuel arriving just as he finished.

"You acted foolishly," Samuel said. "You have not kept the command the Lord your God gave you; if you had, he would have established your kingdom over Israel for all time. But now your kingdom will not endure; the Lord has sought out a man after his own heart and appointed him leader of his people, because you have not kept the Lord's command" (1 Samuel 13:13-14).

This is a tough one, isn't it? I must confess I may very well have fallen into the same trap that Saul did. Surrounded by the enemy with his troops deserting him, he must have been thinking God made a mistake in His command. Either that or maybe he thought the Lord had forgotten about him. He did what most of us probably would have to admit is our own personal instinct: He took matters into his own hands.

How about you? Have you been faced with circumstances where it just didn't seem to make practical sense to do what is right in God's eyes? Maybe a little exaggeration to win a big order? How about overlooking an accounting error in your favor? Or spreading rumors about a competitor? When crisis hits in business, is our first reaction to get on our knees in prayer or to take the bull by the horns ourselves? Isn't there a lot of Saul in all of us?

Obedience Beats Sacrifice

Unfortunately, Saul still had not learned his lesson. Told to destroy totally the Amalekites, including all their livestock, he held back the choice sheep and livestock to sacrifice to God. It was as if He was deluded into thinking he knew better than God and could please Him even with willful disobedience.

When Samuel confronted him again, Saul made excuses. Samuel would have none of it. "Does the Lord delight in burnt offerings and sacrifices as much as in obeying the voice of the Lord? To obey is better than sacrifice, and to heed is better than the fat of rams. For rebellion is like the sin of divination, and arrogance like the evil of idolatry. Because you have rejected the word of the Lord, he has rejected you as king" (1 Samuel 15:22-23).

What a horrifying indictment! Do you justify bad behavior, thinking the end justifies the means? God cannot be honored by disobedience, rebellion and sin.

While serving in Uganda, I became friends with a Christian who had been permanently disabled on the job. Rather than compensating for his loss, the company he worked for fired him instead. My friend hired a lawyer. What should have been a clear cut case dragged on for years in the corrupt Uganda legal system. Hearing after hearing was scheduled and then canceled.

Convinced someone was getting paid off, I took my friend with me to visit a powerful and politically connected Christian Ugandan lawyer I had come to know. The new lawyer took one look at my friend's files and said a settlement of about $6,000 (a lot of money in Uganda) already had been ordered. It just needed to be enforced by the court. He said he could get the money in 30 days and, as a courtesy to me, would not charge a fee.

There was one catch. He needed about $300 for "tips" (Ugandan euphemism for bribes) for court workers to get the case on the docket. "I don't know if we can do that," I said as I left with my disappointed friend. On the way out of the office, the conviction of the Lord hit me and I said to my friend, "If you paid a bribe, received all $6,000 and gave every bit of it to the church, would God be pleased?"

He didn't hesitate with his one word answer, "No." Case closed.

"Like a partridge that hatches eggs it did not lay is the man who gains riches by unjust means. When his life is half gone, they will desert him, and in the end he will prove to be a fool" (Jeremiah 17:11).

Lying to God

Annanias and Sapphira are a tragic couple in the Book of Acts who may have set out to do the right thing but then botched it big-time.

Annanias sold a piece of property and gave it to the apostles for the church. However, with Sapphira's full knowledge but no one else's, Annanias kept back part for himself, leaving a false impression in the church. The Holy Spirit revealed the ruse through Peter. "What made you think of doing such a thing?" Peter asked. "You have not lied to me but to God."

Annanias fell dead and shortly thereafter, his wife Sapphira did as well. The Bible reports this sent great fear through the church. We could do with more fear of the Lord today ourselves.

Once again, God demonstrates that our motives, or heart condition, override our actions. This story also is a telling reminder that nothing we do is hidden from God's sight (Hebrews 4:13) and that He will not be mocked (Galatians 6:7).

I am continually amazed at how people who consider themselves committed Christians often choose to make compromises to please man rather than God.

I remember driving one night on a winding, hilly road with two successful businessmen who had chosen to delegate many of the duties related to their business and spend a great deal of time in missions and ministry themselves. One of them related a story about a dilemma faced by close family friends. The friends had a bright son who had recently finished high school with good grades and been accepted to a fine university.

The problem was the parents learned the son had cheated on his final exams to secure his rank in the graduating class and acceptance to his university of choice. The parents opted to keep quiet.

To my great dismay, my two businessman friends defended the parents' decision to cover up the cheating. "If they told the school, that could destroy his whole life," one of the businessmen said. They were adamant about it and offended by my indignation at the choice to cover the boy's sin. The truth is they were all deceived thinking that hiding the sin would avoid negative impacts. God knows all and He is just.

Also, what were the parents teaching this young man? They taught him that cheating is okay if you get what you want and that fear of man is greater than fear of God. This sounds to me like a message straight from hell.

I suppose that I should not have been surprised when some time later I learned the two businessman friends also had overlooked serious sin by a ministry leader. Although they warned the leader for his indiscretions, they failed to take action. Only when the leader was exposed by someone else (and after more people had been harmed and betrayed by his actions) did he face the consequences of being removed from his position.

As the saying goes, we can run but we cannot hide. We all give an account to God. A healthy fear of God is a great thing.

The Good News

So what is the antidote for our "deceitful" hearts? Jesus is the cure.

"So I find this law at work: When I want to do good, evil is right there with me. For in my inner being I delight in God's law; but I see another law at work in the members of my body, waging war against the law of my mind and making me a prisoner of the law of sin at work within my members. What a wretched man I am! Who will rescue me from this body of death? Thanks be to God – through Jesus Christ our Lord! So then, I myself in my mind am a slave to God's law, but in the sinful nature a slave to the law of sin" (Romans 7:21-25).

As Jesus instructed his disciples in the story of the rich young ruler, what is impossible for man is possible for God. And, as believers in Jesus, we have the spirit of the Holy God within us! It is that spirit in our heart that allows us to overcome the sinful cravings in our hearts.

Paul put it this way:

"Therefore, there is now no condemnation for those who are in Christ Jesus, because through Christ Jesus the law of the Spirit of life set me free from the law of sin and death. For what the law was powerless to do in that it was weakened by the sinful nature, God did by sending his own Son in the likeness of sinful man to be a sin offering. And so he condemned sin in sinful man, in order that the righteous requirements of the law might be fully met in us, who do not live according to the sinful nature but according to the Spirit. Those who live according to the sinful nature have their minds set on what that nature desires; but those who live in accordance with the Spirit have their minds set on what the Spirit desires. The mind of sinful man is death, but the mind controlled by the Spirit is life and peace; the sinful mind is hostile to God. It does not submit to God's law, nor can it do so. Those controlled by the sinful nature cannot please God.

"You, however, are controlled not by the sinful nature but by the Spirit, if the Spirit of God lives in you. And if anyone does not have the Spirit of Christ, he does not belong to Christ. But if Christ is in you, your body is dead because of sin, yet your spirit is alive because of righteousness.

And if the Spirit of him who raised Jesus from the dead is living in you, he who raised Christ from the dead will also give life to your mortal bodies through his Spirit, who lives in you.

"Therefore, brothers, we have an obligation – but it is not to the sinful nature, to live according to it. For if you live according to the sinful nature, you will die; but if by the Spirit you put to death the misdeeds of the body, you will live, because those who are led by the Spirit of God are sons of God" (Romans 8:1-14).

More Than Conquerors

Are you "led by the Spirit of God" or are you led by worldly standards and selfish desires? If you are led by the Spirit of God, nothing can stand against you.

"No, in all these things we are more than conquerors through him who loved us" (Romans 8:38).

We are not immune from temptation or troubles, but we are given the power to overcome them. Jesus said: "I have told you these things, so that in me you may have peace. In this world you will have trouble. But take heart! I have overcome the world" (John 16:33).

Notice Jesus' reference to overcoming the world is in the past tense. If He is in our heart, we already have overcome trials through Him! As a believer, you are made to be an overcomer!

The only catch is you must call upon the power of Jesus within you to be victorious. Sometimes we simply take things on ourselves and neglect calling out to the Lord for His strength, guidance and wisdom. Other times we specifically refuse to call upon Him because we want to satisfy the desires of our flesh and indulge in ungodly behavior.

An example is a friend of mine who struggled with pornography. To his credit, he shared his problem with a couple of close Christian friends and asked for prayer.

But, when I asked if, when tempted, he prayed at that moment and asked God for strength to overcome the sinful desire, he responded he did not. The reason was at the moment of temptation he loved the sin more than he loved God. He knew if he called upon the Lord to overcome he would receive strength to do so, yet he would not.

God's Love Language

As noted earlier, Jesus tells us we can best express our love to Him through obedience. From this perspective, we should look upon every temptation as an opportunity to show our love for Him! When we call upon Him to overcome sin and remain obedient through His power, we are speaking His love language.

Every time we snatch a "white lie" or exaggeration from the tip of our tongue and every time we reject coarse talk, anger, jealousy, envy, pride and dishonest gain, we are expressing an act of love to our Lord.

And every time we show love to the Lord this way we are making a radical statement that we serve Him and not the standards of a fallen world.

Obedience to the Lord is the greatest testimony we can give to Him. As Saint Francis of Assisi said long ago, "Preach the gospel everywhere you go, and, if necessary, use words." By your obedience and example, you will be a recognizable force for the Lord in the business world and elsewhere.

If your business associates do not know you are a Christian unless you tell them, you may need to do some serious self examination. Jesus is radical and if you are living for Him it can't help but show.

Take the example of Zacchaeus in Luke Chapter 19. He was a despised and corrupt chief tax collector. Still, he was so excited to see Jesus when He arrived in town that, being a short man, he climbed a tree to see Him. Jesus spotted him and invited Himself to Zacchaeus' house.

"All the people saw this and began to mutter, 'He has gone to be the guest of a 'sinner.' But Zacchaeus stood up and said to the Lord, 'Look, Lord! Here and now I give half of my possessions to the poor, and if I have cheated anybody out of anything, I will pay back four times the amount.'

"Jesus said to him, 'Today salvation has come to this house, because this man, too, is a son of Abraham. For the Son of Man came to seek and to save what was lost'" (Luke 19:7-9).

The change in Zacchaeus was radical and undeniable. He surrendered to Jesus, saw his sins through the newly found conviction in his heart and took action immediately to address his wrongdoings.

There was no doubt of his master to anyone. Can the same be said for you?

If not, take the spiritual heart exam. Claim Jesus as the cure for your condition. Get in the Word. Get on your knees. Get your priorities straight. Do business God's way.

Chapter 1: What is the Condition of Your Heart?

Discussion Questions

1. What does it mean to know "the condition of your heart?" Give examples.

2. What can get your heart in top "spiritual condition?"

3. Discuss specific types of "spiritual plaque" that cause a slow blockage between God and you.

4. Give practical examples of our desire to be in control (Lord of our lives), instead of following God's plan which leads to peace.

5. Discuss the types of decisions and motives that lead to a diseased spiritual heart. Can we relate to Saul?

6. What ways can we show God we love Him in all our decisions? Discuss bribes. Are they ever justified?

7. What is the cure for "deceitful" hearts? Why do we lie to God?

8. Define spiritual death. Discuss obedience and its relationship to restoration.

Personal Reflection

1. Are there unhealthy habits over the years that are impacting the condition of my heart and developing "spiritual plaque?" Lord reveal any habit that is impacting my heart.

2. What specific things can I do through the day to increase the "spiritual health" of my heart? Pray for the Lord to guide and bring things to mind that will help.

3. Do I frequently choose to make compromises to please man rather than God?

4. Is there any rebelliousness in my heart?

5. Do I feel guilty or in bondage without a feeling of peace? Do people know who is my master by my actions?

Chapter 2
Let Your Yes Be Yes and Your No Be No

"Simply let your 'Yes' be 'Yes,' and your 'No,' 'No'; anything beyond this comes from the evil one" (Matthew 5:37).

With these simple yet powerful words, Jesus raised the bar from the Ten Commandments against lying: "You shall not give false testimony against your brother" (Deuteronomy 5:20).

No longer is it just about the absence of lying in the moment, it is about your commitment to follow through. "I do" is a "yes," even though a Barna Group study in 2008 showed that 26 percent of all evangelical Christian adults in the U.S. have been divorced. Their "yes" did not turn out not to be "yes" after all.[1]

George Barna, who directed the study, noted that Americans have grown comfortable with divorce as a natural part of life.

"There no longer seems to be much of a stigma attached to divorce; it is now seen as an unavoidable rite of passage," the researcher indicated. "Interviews with young adults suggest that they want their initial marriage to last, but are not particularly optimistic about that possibility. There is also evidence that many young people are moving toward embracing the idea of serial marriage, in which a person gets married two or three times, seeking a different partner for each phase of their adult life."

Personally, I also have witnessed a younger generation that seems to have trouble making commitments and keeping them. Even for something as simple as a dinner party or small group church gathering, I have seen many change plans at the last minute for a "better offer."

In explaining my long term discipleship ministry to a 20-something professional, the fellow believer told me the concept was difficult to convey

---

1   Barna, George. *The Barna Update*, March 2008

to her generation because they preferred to move from one experience to the next rather than make long term commitments.

The Scripture enlightens us that when your "yes" is really a "no" we have been manipulated by the evil one. Think of the practical, emotional and spiritual fall out of divorce among men, women and children.

Tearing apart our families is a favorite target of Satan. As the "father of lies" (John 8:44) Satan also seeks to tinge the truth and erode our fidelity in other interpersonal and business relationships.

We expect politicians to lie – many even marveled at former President Bill Clinton's ability to "spin" the truth. "It depends on what the meaning of the word is, is," as he said in his grand jury testimony regarding the Monica Lewinsky scandal. [2] His further contention in front of the grand jury that fellatio did not constitute sex emboldened a generation of teenagers to imitate his behavior.

Lying and misrepresentation from Enron and WorldCom executives early in the new millennium led to disgrace, collapse, and ruin for those companies and their leaders. Falsities can have the same impact on us.

"White Lies" Are Dark

Our society seems to have embraced the notion that "white lies" are okay. Like calling in sick. I have seen advertising campaigns urging people to call in sick to attend baseball games and other activities. Lying to decline an undesired invitation is commonplace.

I remember as a manager of a sales team, I requested a budget to conduct team building events. I was told there was no budget for that, but that I should pay for the events myself and then inflate my automobile mileage on my expense report to get reimbursement.

Being a young Christian at the time, I did not think and followed the suggested procedure. A year later, the Holy Spirit showed me that not only was I lying, but I also could be charged with stealing. More than that, I was offending God.

"Against you, you only, have I sinned and done what is evil in your sight, so that you are proved right when you speak and justified when you judge" (Psalm 51:4).

I stopped the practice, repented and prayed for forgiveness. We had to do without the team building.

Any sin is an offense to God, of course, but beyond that, the "white lies" form a pattern which, if not checked by the Holy Spirit within us, lead to bigger, more complex and injurious lies and falsities with ugly consequences. As Sir Walter Scott[3] wrote, "Oh what a tangled web we weave, when first we practice to deceive."

Jesus is telling us to keep it simple but the master of confusion (the devil) is exploiting our selfish, greedy and prideful desires to muck things up.

A Simple Example

Our Western world has turned deception into an intricate art form, so I like to share a simple example from my teaching to business people in Africa. The story is based on actual events I experienced and similar transactions occur daily. The practices and impacts of the story are universal.

Suppose you are a carpenter with your own small shop. A customer (let's call him William) comes to request that you make a desk for him. William likes your work; you agree on a price. He is willing to pay you a deposit for the materials; his only requirement is that you complete the piece in seven days.

You know you already have a backlog of work and it will be highly unlikely you can complete the job in seven days without further delaying other customers whose deadlines you already have missed. Still, you need the cash from the deposit so you promise to complete the desk in seven days.

Perhaps when you make the commitment you acknowledge to yourself that there is no way you can complete the job on time. Or perhaps you choose to overlook that fact and think by some miracle you will be able to clear all your backlog and complete the job as promised. Either way, you are falling short of an important Biblical business principle: planning by counting the cost.

---

3   Scott, Sir Walter. *Marmion, Canto* vi. Stanza 17.

"Suppose one of you wants to build a tower. Will he not first sit down and estimate the cost to see if he has enough money to complete it? For if he lays the foundation and is not able to finish it, everyone who sees it will ridicule him, saying, 'This fellow began to build and was not able to finish.'

"Or suppose a king is about to go to war against another king. Will he not first sit down and consider whether he is able with ten thousand men to oppose the one coming against him with twenty thousand? If he is not able, he will send a delegation while the other is still a long way off and will ask for terms of peace" (Luke 14:28-31).

Jesus in these verses is talking about the cost of being a disciple, but the concept of counting the cost is transferable to all we do in keeping our commitments and making sure our yes is indeed yes.

Choosing to be ignorant of our circumstance or capacity to deliver goes against the Biblical concept of counting the cost of our decisions. Willfully misrepresenting our ability to deliver demonstrates ignorance of the consequences of not counting the cost.

Back to our example of the desk, let's see how the consequences play out. The delivery date of the desk is due and you have not even begun to start on it. As a matter of fact, you even had used the deposit for the desk to finish off the materials for a dining set for another customer who also was hounding you because his order was two weeks late.

William the hopeful customer appears to collect his desk. He is not happy when he sees you have not even begun work on it. You promise to have it in five more days to calm William down, even though you have no idea now where you will get the money to buy the materials even if you had the time to work on the desk.

Five days later, you have notified your assistant to keep an eye out for William. You plan to stay in the back of the shop and run away and hide when he returns as you still have not begun work on the desk. When William arrives, your assistant tells him you are not in – that you were called out of town to attend the funeral of a family member.

And so it goes. One lie builds on top of another. You are fearful of William and looking over your shoulder constantly to make sure he doesn't spot you. William now is telling everyone in his path of his bad experience with you and urging that other customers avoid your business by all means.

Hopefully, you have never been in either William's shoes or the carpenter's shoes, but probably you can relate to some of the aspects of this disaster.

In your career or business, have you ever made a commitment without counting the cost? Have you ever been dazzled by the prospect of getting an order into promising delivery times or features you could not provide? Have you ever robbed Peter to pay Paul? Have you ever avoided someone you had let down?

Can you see Jesus' wisdom in telling us to let our yes be yes and no be no? Do you understand how Satan uses our failure to follow the Word to divide and conquer?

When Things Don't Work Out as Planned

My wife Margaret and I once owned a business that failed. It was ugly. We were unable to meet financial commitments and people got hurt. I'm sure some of them would be appalled that I would presume to address the topic of Doing Business God's Way.

I have no excuses. When we started the incentive travel and destination management business, I was not yet a believer in Jesus and my wife was a slumbering infant in the Lord who had been born again on a high school ski trip but never discipled.

We never sought the Lord's guidance in launching and managing the business until, about three years in, God used a crisis with our daughter Audrey to get our attention and gather us all to Himself. Almost immediately, the Holy Spirit began spotlighting ungodly aspects of our business to us. We made changes and surrendered it to Him, getting baptized by immersion together as a family. (We all had been sprinkled as infants).

About a year later, the business simply ran out of gas. We had a boom and bust cycle that was tied somewhat to a fickle travel market. Still, I remember earlier as an unbeliever sitting on the front steps of our home under a sky full of stars. We were at a critical point – like in a poker game when you need to make a decision to fold or put all your chips in the pot. In my head, I knew we should fold. But I had dodged too many bullets in prior successful business ventures before and convinced myself we were smart enough to make things work. I laid out the scenarios to Margaret.

We decided to go for it. Wrong choice.

No One Sets Out to Fail

Of course, we never intended to fail. But we did. I think had we been active believers earlier, we probably never would have started that type of business. Nevertheless, we were not immune to consequences of prior bad choices when we came to know the Lord.

If you are a believer, you have a powerful weapon I did not have when we started that business. You have the Holy Spirit and the offer of wisdom if you ask for it. "If any of you lacks wisdom, he should ask God, who gives generously without finding fault and it will be given to him" (James 1:5).

Of course, receiving wisdom is not necessarily the same thing as listening to it and acting on it. Sometimes we want what we want when we want it. We rely upon our own strength and determination. Isn't this the American dream: being a self-made business person who "pulled himself up by his bootstraps?"

Certainly many enterprising persons have succeeded spectacularly in building companies relying on their own intelligence, determination and strength.

But beware. According to Illusions of Entrepreneurship: The Costly Myths That Entrepreneurs, Investors and Policy Makers Live By, written by Scott Shane, 55 percent of all U.S. start up businesses fail within the first five years and 71 percent fail by year 10.[4] None of these businesses set out to fail, so perhaps it is wise to consider that determination and, yes, even faith, are not enough to establish a successful business.

In my work with Christian businessmen, I often run across men who are completely convinced their proposed business will succeed if they just have faith in God that it will. Except for salvation through Jesus, God does not promise us specific results. We must remember that His ways are not our ways (Isaiah 55:9) and that our heart (desire) is deceitful above all things (Jeremiah 17:9).

---

4   Shane, Scott. *Illusions of Entrepreneurship: The Costly Myths That Entrepreneurs, Investors and Policy Makers Live By.* Yale University, 2008

Presumption is Not Faith

Presuming upon God for a specific result is not the same as having faith in God. Romans 8:28 promises: "And we know that in all things God works for the good of those who love him, who have been called according to his purpose." Notice He is not promising we will get what we want; just that if we are "called according to his purpose" that He will work it all out for the good.

Many times we can see no good coming from our failures. But, in truth, do we learn and grow more from our successes or our failures when we are submitted to the Lord?

Another unintentional cause of failing to let our yes be yes and faltering in our commitments is the "counting the cost" principle mentioned in the example about the carpenter. In our ministry, we have had excited supporters cavalierly pledge support which they discovered in a very short time they could not deliver. They meant well; they just had not thought things through.

Of course, there also are times when people do everything right biblically, but circumstances change and they simply cannot keep their commitments. Perhaps you lose your job through no fault of your own and are unable to afford your mortgage payment. If you are in a "down" real estate market, you might not be able to sell it for a sufficient price to pay off your mortgage. This is not uncommon.

God does call us at times to show our love and obedience to Him by sticking with our commitments even against our strong personal desires. The earlier discussion of marriage is an example. Jesus provides only two valid reasons for divorce: adultery by your spouse or abandonment by an unbelieving spouse. This is tough teaching in a culture where the main desire is to please ourselves rather than God. My wife Margaret and I have seen God do great things in troubled marriages, however, when people seek to please God by honoring their commitments to Him and persevering in their vows rather than satisfying their own desires to flee or find another mate.

When our yes can no longer be yes, how can we still please God? First, if you are at fault, confess to the Lord. Repent. Learn your lesson. Change your behavior.

Regardless of whether your changed circumstances are a result of your actions or apparently unavoidable, be truthful and forthcoming to those whom you are unable to keep your commitments. Tell them the whole truth. Seek their mercy and forgiveness. Perhaps you can work out a plan which will help you meet your commitments, even partially, over time.

You can give honor and glory to God even in confronting your failures. "The sacrifices of God are a broken spirit; a broken and contrite heart, O God, you will not despise" (Psalms 51:17).

We can take heart that God forgives our missed promises and even revels in restoring us to do great things. Peter is a perfect example. He declared he would never disown Jesus, yet did so that very night. Still, Peter was forgiven and Jesus fulfilled His promise:

"And I tell you that you are Peter, and on this rock I will build my church, and the gates of Hades will not overcome it I will give you the keys of the kingdom of heaven; whatever you bind on earth will be bound in heaven, and whatever you loose on earth will be loosed in heaven" (Matthew 16:18-19).

Is It Ever Okay to Lie?

If someone is looking for an excuse to lie, they certainly could take biblical examples out of context and make a case.

Consider Abraham who lied to Pharaoh (Genesis 12:10-13) and King Abimelech (Genesis 20:1-2), claiming his wife Sarah was his sister instead. Abraham feared he would be killed so the men could claim Sarah for themselves if they knew she was his wife. The Bible does not condone this lie, it merely reports it. We do not know what the result would have been if Abraham had trusted God in the matter.

Then there is the case of Rahab, a prostitute in Jericho who lied to protect the spies sent by Joshua ahead of the Israelites' conquest of the city. Not only is she honored in the Bible (Hebrews 11:31), but God even chose her to be in the lineage of Jesus (Matthew 1:5)!

Deception remains a key part of warfare to this day.

Jacob, who was renamed Israel and is the namesake for the nation, was a classic con artist. He deceived his father Isaac and cheated his brother

Esau out of his father's blessing and inheritance (Genesis Chapter 27).

Then there is the puzzling time God sent a "lying spirit" to the prophets of Ahab to spell disaster for him. (2 Chronicles 18:22)

Perhaps these examples are beyond our understanding of God's character. However, none of these examples provides any justification for falsities in our daily lives.

Chapter 2: Let Your Yes Be Yes and Your No Be No

Discussion Questions

1. Discuss why you think the Bible tells us to "let your yes be yes and your no be no"?

2. What is the practical application of Luke 24:28-31?

3. What are some examples of ways to implement this discipline in your life?

4. God reports lies in the Bible, but doesn't condone them. Consider and discuss how "white lies" impact our witness as believers and modeling behavior for our family members. Discuss how white lies begin a pattern of behavior.

5. How does this principle impact the development of mutual respect and trust? Discuss how this truth impacts marriage.

6. Does God ever promise specific results? How does presuming on God differ from having faith?

Personal Reflection

1. What ways can I be alert to temptation and manipulation of Satan?

2. Reflect on personal consequences pertaining to telling lies in my career.

3. Do I always count the costs before making a commitment?

4. Have I asked God's guidance in my business decisions?

5. Think about a time when a failure taught me something. Did I see God's hand in what was going on?

Chapter 3
Accountable

"Nothing in all creation is hidden from God's sight. Everything is uncovered and laid bare before the eyes of him to whom we must give account" (Hebrews 4:13).

Whether you know it or not – or whether you like it or not – you are accountable.

The only question is whether you allow the Lord and others to speak into your heart now while you have a chance to conform to Christ's likeness on earth or whether you wait to see your faults replayed at judgment day before your Maker (Revelation 20:11).

Secular Accountability

The lack of accountability in the business world by such companies as Enron and WorldCom caused a tremor in the economy and action by Congress in 2002.

The Sarbanes-Oxley Act established strict compliance guidelines in corporate governance, securities analysis and performance of audits.

A primary goal of the law was to guarantee awareness and provide accountability of company directors and officers regarding their financial affairs. Most public companies were required to have an audit committee to oversee closely the operations of the auditing firm retained. CEOs and CFOs were personally mandated to certify company financial disclosures and controls. It became a federal crime for company officers to pressure auditors to manipulate data.

The law also outlawed most loans to company officials and prohibited officers and directors from trading their company's securities when other employees or retirement-plan participants are not allowed to do so.

Whistleblower protections were extended to employees and stricter conflict of interest measures were put in place. The necessary law was the result of a fallen corporate world where top officers sheltered themselves from accountability.

Spiritual Accountability

I believe spiritual accountability encouraged by churches and Christian organizations today frequently resembles the type of secular accountability laid out in laws like Sarbanes-Oxley. Basically, we have a set of checklists and "don'ts" that we report to fellow Christians.

Rather than spurring one another on to good deeds and a closer relationship with the Lord, we are "high fiving" one another for following the law and avoiding bad deeds.

Here is a list of "sample accountability questions" from MenOfIntegrity. org, preceded by the reminder, "Regardless of the accountability questions you choose, the last question should be 'Have you been truthful about everything we have discussed?'[5]

-Have you spent time with God on a regular basis?
- Have you compromised your integrity in any way?
- Has your thought life been pure?
- Have you committed any sexual sin?
- How much time did you spend in prayer this week?
- Did you pray for the others in this group?
- Did you put yourself in an awkward situation with a woman?
- What one sin plagued your walk with God this week?
- Did you accomplish your spiritual goals this week?
- Are you giving to the Lord's work financially?
- How have you demonstrated a servant's heart?
- Do you treat your peers and coworkers as people loved by God?
- What significant thing did you do for your wife and/or family?
- What was your biggest disappointment? How did you decide to handle it?
- What was your biggest joy? Did you thank God?
- What do you see as your number one need for next week?
- Are you satisfied with the time you spent with the Lord this week?

5   www.menofintegrity.org, *Sample Accountability Questions*, 2008.

- Did you take time to show compassion for others in need?
- Did you control your tongue?
- What did you do this week to enhance your relationship with your spouse and/or child(ren)?
- Did you pray and read God's Word this week? What did you derive from this time?
- In what ways have you stepped out in faith since we last met?
- In what ways has God blessed you this week? And what disappointments consumed your thoughts this week?
- Did you look at a woman in the wrong way?
- How have you been tempted this week? How did you respond?
- How has your relationship with Christ been changing?
- Did you worship in church this week?
- Have you shared your faith this week? How?
- What are you wrestling with in your thought life?
- What have you done for someone else this week?
- Are the "visible" you and the "real" you consistent?

It's About Being

I don't know about you, but that list wears me out! I believe the Christian life is about "being" rather than "doing." Being in a close relationship with the Lord is an intimate, personal matter to be done out of love and reverence for Him, not out of fear of what answers I will have for my buddies at my next 6 a.m. breakfast with them. Men, in particular, often prefer checklists over relationships. But the whole reason Jesus came down from heaven to earth to die on a cross was so we could have an eternal relationship with Him in heaven.

As noted earlier, Jesus says those who love Him will obey Him (John 14:15). As we love Him, we decrease and He increases within us. (John 3:30). The result is our cup overflows with Him (Psalm 23:5). It is only through the power of the Holy Spirit that we are able to obey Him. "But the Counselor, the Holy Spirit, whom the Father will send in my name, will teach you all things and will remind you of everything I have said to you" (John 14:26).

My point here is not that accountability is not important, but rather that spiritual accountability should not be about checklists.

Sometimes, as leaders and successful business people, we forget who we serve and begin to believe the accolades of those subordinates and others who have a vested interest in flattering us. Or, like King David, we fall into a trap believing our desires are paramount.

David saw a beautiful woman, Bathsheba, bathing from his rooftop and claimed her as his own by calling her to his bed even though she was married. He compounded the sin by arranging for the death of her husband, Uriah. Amazingly, he appeared oblivious to his sin until it was tactfully pointed out by his friend Nathan.

To his credit, David's response was immediate: "I have sinned against the Lord" (2 Samuel 12:13). The consequence was that the son born to David and Bathsheba from the illicit interlude died.

Remorse Over Sin or Getting Caught?

Still, God called David a "man after his own heart" (Acts 13:22) not because of his failures, but because of his readiness to confess his sins and seek repentance. I have seen many people who appeared contrite not because they had "sinned against the Lord," but rather because they had been caught.

We all need a Nathan. Studies have shown the #1 reason pastors fall into sexual sin is they become isolated and lack a Nathan. Isolation tends to breed self absorption. Fellowship with believing peers reminds us that we are servants of the Lord, not masters of ourselves or our flock. We are to serve rather than be served (Matthew 20:28).

We need to encourage one another to grow in intimacy with the Lord. We need to fellowship with other believers. We need to sing songs of praise and worship together. We need to tell of His triumphs in our life and share our burdens together. We need to pray together. We need to be in the Word together – not studying the latest "five points on being a better Christian" – but in the Bible itself expecting Him to speak directly to us and sharing what He is telling us.

We need to encourage one another to allow the Lord to take a flashlight and shine it in the dark corners of our hearts that we do not even want to acknowledge to ourselves. We need to be still and know that He is God (Psalms 46:10). We need to become overcomers through Jesus (John 16:33).

Doesn't this sound richer than responding to a list of questions every week? And shouldn't we fear God rather than man? (Proverbs 29:25). So, accountability groups, be loosed! Enjoy the fruits of your salvation. Show Jesus in you. He will fill you up if you surrender to Him. Claim the power of the Holy Spirit and boldly proclaim His marvelous deeds among one another.

Implications for Business

When we are in a close relationship with the Lord, the Holy Spirit checks us when we are tempted to succumb to ungodly business practices.

When a vendor mistakenly undercharges us, or a customer inadvertently overpays us, the Holy Spirit prompts us to do the right thing. Each temptation to slip presents an opportunity to express our love to Him by doing the right thing. This also can provide a powerful witness for the Lord if we express our honesty as being a result of being accountable to the Lord and loving Him.

Our primary accountability partner is Jesus. Unlike the guys we like to talk sports with as well as go through our list of accountability questions, Jesus is actually there at our moment of temptation. He is able to give us strength to overcome the temptation and knows instantly if we don't.

I have never known anyone who prayed at the moment of temptation to overcome it and failed to do so. I had a friend who struggled with pornography. I asked him if he prayed for restraint when tempted. He responded negatively. The truth is he loved the sin more than he loved the Lord at the moment of temptation. He failed to pray because he knew the Lord would honor his prayer and he wanted to indulge his flesh more than he wanted to show his love to the Lord through obedience.

The same is true in business temptations. You have the power of the Lord but, like a light switch, it does you no good unless you turn it on.

You are only fooling yourself if you think you can escape accountability. "Do not be deceived: God cannot be mocked. A man reaps what he sows. The one who sows to please his sinful nature, from that nature will reap destruction; the one who sows to please the Spirit, from the Spirit will reap eternal life" (Galatians 6:7-8).

Chapter 3: Accountable

Discussion Questions

1. Discuss your thoughts about secular versus spiritual accountability.

2. Think about your decisions and who are you accountable to and influenced by as you make them. Is Jesus your primary accountability partner? Explain how He came to be the One.

3. Discuss how checklists can be a hindrance in our relationships with Jesus.

4. What are some of the challenges of isolation when you are in leadership?

5. What are some dangerous pitfalls when leaders surround themselves with "yes men or women?"

Personal Reflection

1. Am I an "overcomer" as in John 16:33 when faced with temptations?

2. Does my relationship with the Lord have an impact on accountability?

3. Think about when my relationship with the Lord began and how it has impacted my decisions.

4. Reflect on the biggest temptations in my life.

5. Think about how prayer helps overcome temptations. Try it when you are in a difficult situation and see how it works.

Chapter 4
Faithful

"A faithful man will be richly blessed, but one eager to get rich will not go unpunished" (Proverbs 28:20).

Faithfulness goes to the very essence of the character of God. Can you imagine a day when the sun did not rise? Can you imagine God reneging on His promises? Or changing His mind and revoking your salvation through faith in Jesus?

If we are to be conformed to the likeness of Jesus (Romans 8:29); that likeness must radiate faithfulness. His faithfulness is so reassuringly emphasized throughout the Scriptures.

"Jesus Christ is the same yesterday and today and forever" (Hebrews 13:8).

"The works of his hands are faithful and just; all his precepts are trustworthy. They are steadfast forever and ever, done in faithfulness and uprightness" (Psalm 111:7-8).

"For the word of the Lord is right and true; he is faithful in all he does" (Psalm 33:4).

"If we confess our sins, he is faithful and just and will forgive us our sins and purify us from all unrighteousness" (1 John 1:9). Praise Him for his faithfulness!

God is faithful to Himself and us because that is His nature. That same nature to be true to God's Word lives in the believer through the Holy Spirit, but sometimes in business we suppress it to achieve our own selfish desires. We may be faithful to the bottom line over the Lord; faithful to the "Almighty Dollar"; faithful to personal ambition; faithful to ungodly business partners; faithful to dishonest customers. We can become double-minded – not a good thing.

"My heart is set on keeping your decrees to the very end. I hate double-minded men, but I love your law" (Psalms 119:112-113).

When No One is Looking

Our faithfulness also is defined by what we do when no other person is looking. Will we steal if we think we can get away with it? (Even taking a ream of paper from the office or a box of pens?)

Do we succumb to pornography late at night after everyone has gone to bed? If so, we are being faithful to our flesh and the devil, not the Lord. However, it is folly to think we are getting away with it: "There is nothing concealed that will not be disclosed, or hidden that will not be made known. What you have said in the dark will be heard in the daylight, and what you have whispered in the ear in the inner rooms will be proclaimed from the roofs" (Luke 12:2-3).

The cliché of "When the cat's away, the mice will play" was tragically illustrated when Moses went up to Mount Sinai to receive the Ten Commandments.

"Then the Lord said to Moses, "Go down, because your people, whom you brought up out of Egypt, have become corrupt. They have been quick to turn away from what I commanded them and have made themselves an idol cast in the shape of a calf. They have bowed down to it and sacrificed to it and have said, 'These are your gods, O Israel, who brought you up out of Egypt'" (Exodus 32:7).

How quick we are to turn away from God and take matters into our own hands during times of difficulty and uncertainty! Despite their miraculous escape from slavery in Egypt and witnessing the parting of the sea, allowing them to cross before the enemy was swallowed up, the Jews chose to forget God's previous faithfulness to them in favor of a stupid golden calf!

One of the best ways to remain faithful to God is to remind ourselves of how He has been faithful to us. "You performed miraculous signs and wonders in Egypt and have continued them to this day, both in Israel and among all mankind, and have gained the renown that is still yours" (Jeremiah 32:20).

As was His custom, Jesus took the concept of faithfulness and raised it another notch in telling the story about the three men each given talents of money (each talent was worth more than $1,000 by today's standards). Faithfulness as illustrated by Jesus in this story is not merely following God's decrees, but also making the most of what He has given us.

In the story in Matthew Chapter 25, a master gives one servant five talents, one servant two talents and the other one talent, each according to his abilities. The first two put the money to work and each doubled their initial amount. They received those words from their master we all long to hear: "Well done, good and faithful servant! You have been faithful with a few things; I will put you in charge of many things. Come and share your master's happiness!"

But the servant given one talent buried his and returned only what had been given to him originally, earning him the title of "wicked, lazy servant." The one talent he returned was taken and given to the servant who had ten.

This story has sobering spiritual and practical applications. Spiritually, we are to multiply by spreading the Good News of free grace, reconciliation with God and eternal life with Him through faith in Jesus. We are not to keep our blessings to ourselves!

God is Looking for a Return

Practically, God expects a return on what He provides. We are to make the most of the gifts we receive. The reason is to give God glory through our best efforts and allow our blessings also to be blessings to others (Genesis 12:2).

I have seen modern day examples of the story of the talents. On the down side, I remember an African ministry that had been blessed with fertile land surrounding mercy homes for children. The ministry asked for and received equipment and seeds to cultivate the land. The crops sprung up, but were not tended. Incredibly, the crops were not even harvested and rotted in the field even though they were only a few steps from the children's homes.

The leader of the ministry asked me if I could assist him in getting additional financial support for the children's homes from churches in the U.S. because the dollars being sent monthly were not enough to purchase items to feed the children. I replied that I could not in good conscience ask for food money for the homes when perfectly good vegetables were rotting right next to them!

On the positive side, a longtime friend of mine has taken faithfulness in honoring God with the blessings given him to new heights. As a primary owner of a funeral home business with a lock on a lucrative market, my friend set his sights on honoring the Lord through excellence.

Inspired by Jim Collins' book *From Good to Great*, my friend embarked on a march to excellence. "I learned that good can be the enemy of great because people can become complacent," he said. "As Christians we shouldn't be satisfied with good."

His business already had a 99 percent customer satisfaction rating, so he took on a more difficult measure: "In terms of what you paid, how would you rate the value of the services received?"

The goal was to increase the "value rating" from 70 percent to 80 percent. The company surpassed the goal ahead of schedule.

Financially, the company had no need to take on such a task, which pushed employees at all levels because of the change and increased accountability required. It pretty much already had saturated the market share.

But spiritually, my friend was making the most of what the Lord had provided him, much to the gratitude of grieving families at the time of their losses.

I have no doubt my friend someday will thrill to hear those words: "Well done, good and faithful servant!"

Chapter 4: Faithful

Discussion Questions

1. Discuss examples of the Holy Spirit's guidance and influence on our lives.

2. What does it mean to be "double-minded? Does this cause confusion? Where does confusion come from?

3. Discuss how we take control instead of turning to God when we have difficulty or uncertainty. Give specific examples.

4. In Matthew 25 Jesus discusses the talents and the concept of faithfulness. Examine and discuss each servant's response when given the task of stewardship.

5. How can we bless others when we are blessed? How does this honor God?

Personal Reflection

1. How do I exhibit faithfulness in my daily life?

2. Is there a difference in people's actions around me when I exhibit faithfulness? (Ex. co-workers, family).

3. Do others know I expect excellence because it honors God in the area of stewardship?

4. Do I justify shortcuts even though I know it isn't right?

5. Reflect on situations where there have been consequences when I took shortcuts that didn't honor God. How did it make me feel?

Chapter 5
Trustworthy

"'Well done, my good servant!' his master replied. 'Because you have been trustworthy in a very small matter, take charge of ten cities'" (Luke 19:17).

The sum of all the other "Attributes of a Godly Business Person" equals trustworthiness.

Without trust, there is no civilization. We trust our bank deposits are safe, we trust the food we eat is untainted, we trust the police to protect us, we trust the airline pilot on the plane we board to get us safely to our destination. Without trust, there is chaos and anarchy.

This type of trust, however, is in a system rather than a person, which differs from the context for the Scripture above from Luke.   Indeed, John Adams, the second U.S. president, is famous for his saying that our country is "a government of laws, and not of men." In effect, it is the laws and oversight that creates trust in the system. We have the FDIC, the FDA, the FAA, etc., to enforce compliance that gives us trust.

Actually, the system assumes people are not trustworthy on their own accord, thus we trust a system that keeps them honest rather than the people themselves. I have seen firsthand countries where the system is corrupt. Police and courts demand bribes, real drugs are stolen and replaced with placebos, foreign aid and treasuries are raided by the powerful and the citizens lose hope. I also know of a ministry whose workers have picked over Christmas presents intended for needy children before they gave them to the intended recipients. This lack of trustworthiness has led to an endless cycle of poverty for underdeveloped nations and is the best evidence that poverty often is first and foremost a spiritual problem rather than a material problem.

Former President Ronald Reagan is famous for his nuclear arms reduction strategy with the former Soviet Union: "Trust, but verify."

Really, is this any trust at all?

We must deal with the fact that we live in a fallen world and that we cannot even trust fellow believers to be immune from sin and temptation. That is why all responsible businesses and ministries have air tight systems of financial controls and accountabilities.

This certainly is not the type of trustworthiness to which Jesus was referring. In God's system, it is the Holy Spirit within us, and the knowledge of the imminent return of Jesus and our accountability to Him, that produces trustworthiness.

The trustworthy verse from Luke at the beginning of this chapter is from the same story in the Book of Matthew used in the earlier discussion of faithfulness. In Matthew, the emphasis is on "faithful," in Luke the focus is on "trustworthy."

In Matthew, the servants who were faithful with "a few things" were put "in charge of many things." In Luke, the ones trustworthy in a "very small matter" were given "charge of ten cities."

Living With Eternity In Mind

Underlying themes of both stories are not only stewardship, faithfulness and trustworthiness, but also accountability and faith. The story tells of a master passing out the talents before he went on a journey. Clearly, the two who multiplied returns on what they were given not only felt accountable for what they received, but they also in fact believed the master would return to see their results. Apparently the third was missing a sense of urgency because he lacked faith the master would return. This points to the return of Jesus. If we believe He will return and we must give an account to Him, we will act differently that if we merely view this is an abstract concept. If we know He is alive and returning, we will be trustworthy. If not, why bother? Are you living as if you will face your Master and be held to account?

This faith in Jesus' return and His ultimate judgment over all, plus our desire to show our love to Him through obedience, should be the motivating factors in each of us for being trustworthy.

Trustworthiness inspires others to believe in you and follow you based on the faithfulness and fidelity you have exhibited in your actions. A good description for trustworthiness is having a "good name."

How do we gain a good name? Proverbs 3:1-4 tells us: "My son, do not forget my teaching, but keep my commands in your heart, for they will prolong your life many years and bring you prosperity. Let love and faithfulness never leave you; bind them around your neck, write them on the tablet of your heart. Then you will win favor and a good name in the sight of God and man."

Proverbs 22:1 adds, "A good name is more desirable than great riches; to be esteemed is better than silver or gold."

A good name, also in business called goodwill, can be measured in monetary amounts. Goodwill can be defined as the value of a business based on expected continued customers and sales, as a result of the venture's name, reputation or other factors. Goodwill can be a significant part of the value of an enterprise.

Passing the Test

I have the delightful testimony of a young man whose business has taken off because of his trustworthiness. Daniel, of Kisumu, Kenya, received "Doing Business God's Way Training" and a no interest loan from the ministry to start his own taxi business.

"The Rock really has changed my life because I've gone through the training of The Rock and, after that, I have changed automatically, completely, because I've got some teaching from Rock like being open, being trustworthy, being faithful and being obedient to God," Daniel said. " It has really helped me so much. Since I came from Rock, I've changed. And I've got a lot of customers – from that!"

He shared that his trustworthiness gained him one loyal German customer who left her debit card with him to pay for repairs on a house in Kenya! "And the account was fat," Daniel said. "That was a test, and I passed."

The Bible gives us several examples of trustworthy men with resulting good names. Joseph is atop my list. After being sold into slavery by his brothers, Joseph was given charge of his master's house and rebuffed the advances of the master's wife. When imprisoned, he was put in charge of the prison. And, when released from prison, he became second only to the Pharaoh in Egypt because of his fidelity and trustworthiness. He did everything as if unto the Lord despite severe injustices, persecutions and trials.

Trust is earned. I like to compare it to a bank account. Each time you are faithful and truthful in a relationship, you make a deposit into your trust account. When you fail, you make a withdrawal. When you overdraw your account, it can be closed – just as a relationship can end when you fail to live up to your commitments consistently.

Trust is the lifeblood of every relationship – whether business, family or marriage. Trust gives us common ground; lack of trust puts up barriers. Trustworthiness is a measure of love; abusing trust and cheating are measures of betrayal.

Becoming trustworthy is a difficult, if not impossible, task to take on yourself. Only one person is worthy of all our trust – Jesus. Everyone else, at one point in time or another, will disappoint.

"May the God of hope fill you with all joy and peace as you trust in him, so that you may overflow with hope by the power of the Holy Spirit" (Romans 15:13).

As we trust in Him, God's hope will overflow with us onto others. He will empower us to be trustworthy.

We must give trust to the One who is trustworthy before we truly can receive it.

"Do not let your hearts be troubled. Trust in God; trust also in me" (John 14:1).

Chapter 5: Trustworthy

Discussion Questions

1. How does trustworthiness impact all of society? Give specific examples in government, banking, payment of bills, spending of money, stock market.

2. Compare consequences of corruption in the U.S. or Western countries versus developing countries.

3. Discuss the impact on individuals in a country when there is a lack of trust. Do you think this impacts poverty? Do you think poverty is a spiritual issue? Why? Give reasons for root causes.

4. Discuss the importance of Proverbs 3:1-5.

5. How does this scripture relate to the "Prosperity Gospel?"

Personal Reflection

1. Does my "condition of my heart" exhibit trustworthiness?

2. Reflect on what others see and comment about your actions and words.

3. Evaluate the meaning of "having a good name."

4. Are my actions consistent so I'm developing a trustworthy reputation in all aspects of my life?

5. Do I have secrets that would damage my good name if exposed?

Chapter 6
Just

"...For he guards the course of the just and protects the way of his faithful ones" (Proverbs 2:8).

Is God fair? If your answer is, "Yes," it might as well be "Hell, yes." Because if that is the case, hell is where we all are going.

Is it fair that God sent His perfect Son to die on a cross for our sins? Of course not. But it is just. When we claim Jesus as the perfect sacrifice for our sins, God's justice is fulfilled by Christ's payment for our transgressions.

Fairness is a human concept; justice is a Kingdom concept. Fairness connotes equal treatment, justice allows mercy and freedom of discernment.

Equality is a basic biblical and democratic concept. God is not a respecter of persons (Acts 10:34). All who trust in Jesus have "the right to become children of God" (John 1:10). God's justice still demands, however, that our sins be covered by the blood of Jesus before we may be in fellowship with Him.

The U.S. Declaration of Independence states, "We hold these truths to be self evident: That all men are created equal and are endowed by their Creator with certain inalienable rights; that among these are life, liberty and the pursuit of happiness."

The issues of equality under the law and mandated employment practices may hinder our ability to place justice over equality. We are expected to treat people in like secular circumstances the same way even if their attitudes are miles apart. This can cause challenges.

For example, in our overseas ministry I have had two key employees who misappropriated funds. (Unfortunately, this is common in impoverished countries where people have not had any funds to manage and thus are ill-equipped to take on financial responsibilities. Realizing it is a sin to tempt someone beyond what they can bear or have experienced, we have instituted controls where employees handle no ministry money directly. This also protects them from desperate friends and relatives who will expect them to give them money if they have access to it and despise them if they don't.)

In the first case of misappropriation of funds, the employee was given a warning after the initial instance and fired after the second. He had no means of making restitution.

In the second case, the employee was suspended after the first instance. After the second instance, he was rebuked, required to confess in front of his peers, apologize to the Board of Directors and make restitution.

The second employee blossomed to become a powerful leader, teacher and role model.

It could be argued these cases were not handled equally and that the first employee was treated unfairly because he was fired and the second one was not.

In each case, I know God gave the wisdom to make the right decision. The first worker was not repentant; the second one was. That was the difference. From a secular point of view, I suppose some would consider that criteria as unfair.

I challenge anyone to show me in the Bible where God says life is supposed to be fair.

The King James Version says "the just shall live by faith" (Romans 1:17). The New International Version uses the word "righteous" instead of "just" for the same passage. The two words are closely linked.

Know God, Love God, Fear God

How can you be just and righteous in your business? It all comes back to Chapter 1, the "condition of your heart." In short, to be just and righteous, you must know God, love God and fear God. Then you will experience the benefits God promises the just and righteous.

Knowing God means being in the Word and in prayer daily. It means worshipping, studying and fellowshipping with other believers.

There are many who know of God, but do not have a relationship with Him. Love is the demonstration of that relationship. As we have emphasized, Jesus says we demonstrate that love for Him through obedience to His Word. Obedience shows a healthy fear of the Lord in the positive sense of the word "fear" as respect. And we know as believers that if we stray from that obedience, we will be disciplined. "Because the Lord disciplines those he loves, as a father the son he delights in" (Proverbs 3:12).

As we know God, love God and fear God we demonstrate His justness and righteousness in us and the benefits are truly amazing.

"Blessed is the man
who does not walk in the counsel of the wicked
or stand in the way of sinners
or sit in the seat of mockers.
But his delight is in the law of the Lord,
and on his law he meditates day and night.
He is like a tree planted by streams of water,
which yields its fruit in season
and whose leaf does not wither.
Whatever he does prospers.
Not so the wicked!
They are like chaff
that the wind blows away.
Therefore the wicked will not stand in the judgment,
nor sinners in the assembly of the righteous.
For the Lord watches over the way of the righteous,
but the way of the wicked will perish." (Psalm 1)

I believe there are some keys to understanding fully this amazing plan. First, notice that God promises the righteous will yield fruit "in season." Who determines the seasons? God, of course. So, in His timing if you are just He will produce fruit from you.

Also, I believe the meaning of "whatever he does prospers" is in the context of Romans 8:28 discussed earlier, "And we know that in all things God works for the good of those who love him, who have been called according to his purpose."

Finally, what an awesome promise: "For the Lord watches over the way of the righteous"! He will guide your steps daily as you commit to doing business His way!

Conversely, the Psalm says, "But the way of the wicked will perish."

The question is, "Which way will you choose as you go about your business every day?"

Chapter 6: Just

Discussion Questions

1. Explain and discuss the difference between being fair and being just.

2. Discuss God's perspective of the concept of equality.

3. Does God treat people differently in the consequences we each receive? Why do you think this happens?

4. Analyze what the U.S. Declaration of Independence says about equality in relation to God, the creator and the meaning of "inalienable rights."

5. Does the "condition of the heart" and a person's repentant actions impact justice spiritually as well as in the secular world? How do you discern the facts of a situation?

Personal Reflection

1. Am I sure I can evaluate the facts of a situation so I can treat a person with justice? How?

2. Through study of what is said in the Bible about righteousness and justice, am I able to clearly discern what to do when faced with a challenge?

3. Think about the process you go through as part of the evaluation.

4. Does what I know about God's character help me understand justice?

5. Think about situations that have required different consequences with different people and how the Bible helped you discern what to do.

Chapter 7
Teachable

"A wise son heeds his father's instruction, but a mocker does not listen to rebuke" (Proverbs 13:1).

The Apostle Paul, formerly called Saul, was learned, but hopelessly unteachable. That is, until he came face-to-face with Jesus on the road to Damascus.

"If anyone else thinks he has reasons to put confidence in the flesh, I have more: circumcised on the eighth day, of the people of Israel, of the tribe of Benjamin, a Hebrew of Hebrews; in regard to the law, a Pharisee; as for zeal, persecuting the church; as for legalistic righteousness, faultless" (Philippians 3:5-6).

On his way to Damascus to imprison Christians, "suddenly a light from heaven flashed around him. He fell to the ground and heard a voice say to him, "Saul, Saul, why do you persecute me?" "Who are you, Lord?" Saul asked. "I am Jesus, whom you are persecuting," he replied. "Now get up and go into the city, and you will be told what you must do'" (Acts 9: 3-6).

Ironically, the defining experience which gave Paul eyes to see blinded him for three days before Jesus anointed him as His ambassador to the Gentiles and Israel alike.

I can relate. God used a radically distressing experience in my life to get my attention and make me teachable. My daughter had run away. The police said runaways often hang out at places like the State Fair, which was taking place at the time. I went to Kinko's, which donated color copies of a picture of my daughter. Then I hit the midway, showing the picture of my daughter to hawkers and carnival workers. It was the low point of my life – I felt I was a failure as a father, husband and businessman. I did not find her on the midway, but the story has a happy ending. A police officer acted outside of policy to report our daughter missing earlier than the standard time. She was found with her boyfriend in the parking lot of a grocery store in our vehicle in a neighboring state. Soon thereafter, she came to know the Lord, which I could not ignore and also acknowledged Jesus as Lord. My wife and I (sprinkled as infants) along with our daughter were baptized together as a family.

(Later, we tried to send a letter of gratitude, using the address on his business card, to the policeman who had filed the missing persons report on our daughter before the standard time. We were told no one by his name had ever worked for the department. My wife believes he is an angel.)

Benefits of Brokenness

"The sacrifices of God are a broken spirit; a broken and contrite heart, O God, you will not despise" (Psalms 51:17). Why do you suppose God values a broken spirit? It is because with the broken spirit we lose our pride and confidence in our flesh and become teachable.

Just as with receiving salvation, it is not mandatory to go through such trauma to become teachable. However, when we harden our hearts we may find God loves us enough to allow us to suffer the consequences of our own actions to reveal our pride and folly.

One of the great dangers of leadership is "operating in a bubble." It is easy for those in positions of authority – whether in business, ministry or elsewhere in the workplace – to surround themselves with those people who will tell them only what they want to hear. In other words, the leader is no longer teachable. Pride requires this type of leader is always right. This reflects not only pride, but insecurity in the leader.

I once was asked to work alongside a ministry for a year and provide constructive advice. I welcomed the opportunity but was disappointed to find my advice and observations were not taken positively. Instead of engaging in discussion, the leader of the ministry took my observations personally and extrapolated them in his mind to have meaning I never intended.

"I know you see evil in all of us and nothing good is anywhere except sin and your letter's attitude and speech shows that it is hard to help us when that is the way you see us," the leader wrote me. "Let us talk and see but I am very hurt by the way you are behaving these days."

I obviously could have communicated more effectively, but the leader of the ministry I am sure was shell shocked by the feedback he sought because he was accustomed to receiving effusive praise, including those who compared him to Nehemiah.

We also have seen in politics and government how leaders can be isolated and develop a myopic view of the world and themselves. Former President Richard Nixon is the prime example.

A biblical example of an unteachable leader who cost his people dearly is Pharaoh. Talk about a guy who just couldn't get it! He refused to listen to God through His messenger Moses even after He turned a staff into a snake, turned Egypt's water to blood, overran the land with frogs, tormented man and beast with overwhelming gnats and flies, sent a plague among the livestock, placed festering boils on men and animals, brought horrendous hailstorms, sent locusts to devour fields and fill houses, and killed the firstborn (man and animal) of the Egyptians.

It is true that God hardened Pharaoh's heart to glorify Himself. But many of us can relate to the hardness, stubbornness and lack of teachability. An example of someone God chose to lead but removed from favor because of his lack of teachability and obedience was Saul, first king of Israel. On the other hand, Saul's successor, David was called "a man after God's own heart," not because he was free from sin, but because he was repentant and teachable.

How Can We Learn if We Won't Listen?

Another great biblical example of someone who was teachable was the Ethiopian eunuch. The Apostle Philip was directed by an angel to the road from Jerusalem to Gaza (Acts 8:26-40).

"Then Philip ran up to the chariot and heard the man reading Isaiah the prophet. "Do you understand what you are reading?" Philip asked. "How can I," he said, "unless someone explains it to me?" So he invited Philip to come up and sit with him." Philip explained; the eunuch believed in Jesus and was baptized.

What if the eunuch, afraid of appearing stupid, had ignored Philip or responded, "Mind your own business," or "No, thank you"? He would not have received salvation at that time.

Fear of appearing ignorant or stupid holds many of us back from being teachable and receiving the instruction and blessings the Lord desires for us. I remember a guideline from Tom Hopkins, a noted author on sales techniques: "Make a fool of yourself at least once per day." The idea is not to be foolish, but to overcome fear of asking questions or doing something out of the ordinary.

Someone I love very dearly and pray for daily who has not acknowledged Jesus' atoning sacrifice as the only way to heaven once revealed to me an underlying reason for the unbelief. "I believed that way when I was young, but when I went to college I changed. I could never go back to what I used to believe." This person's circle of friends is made up of people who deny Jesus is the only way to God. To surrender to Jesus as Savior would make this person foolish in the minds of those friends.

Paul says we are to be "fools for Christ," (1 Corinthians 4:10) meaning we should not fear what the world thinks. In my "Doing Business God's Way" teaching, I tell my students that the only stupid question is the one they do not ask.

Teachable vs. Impressionable

There is a critical distinction between being teachable and being impressionable or gullible. We must be discerning and prayerful in the teaching we embrace. This means measuring it against the Bible, advice of godly friends and good old common sense.

Many of us are looking for "quick fixes" or "five easy steps to _____ (fill in the blank)." One example is in the evangelical churches today where we seem to be reading the books of the hottest authors for life guidance as a substitute for the Word of God. The books are fine as long as they take us back to the Book. Without a strong biblical background, people easily can be led astray by books, whether that is the author's intent or not.

An example is from *Velvet Elvis* by Rob Bell[6]. The book states that "hell is full of forgiven people."

I have debated this statement in a church small group study and it caused much contention and confusion. What would a new believer, or one who does not spend time in the Bible, make of that statement? What

6   Bell, Rob. *Velvet Elvis: Repainting the Christian Faith.* Zondervan, 2006, p. 146.

good is Jesus' sacrifice if forgiven people are in hell?

Yet the book makes the rounds in the churches and I'm sure these confusing statements slip by because Rob Bell is considered a popular pastor and author. This is an example of people being impressionable. Some people when this statement from the book is brought to their attention don't even realize it is in the book. My concern is to be careful what we recommend for small groups to use, especially when new believers or seekers are attending the groups.

I am continually amazed at how people are willing to substitute the truth for a lie (Romans 1:25). For instance, next time you are at a health foods store, take a look at the bulletin board. There you are likely to see announcements for every kind of New Age philosophy and alternative lifestyle that you can imagine. Why is it people will not take the time to examine the claims of Jesus but will eagerly embrace mystical and self-centered faiths?

As Christians, we also must be careful with the latest business trends and books we embrace. One of the students in our ministry became a fan of Donald Trump. Now, The Donald may have some tips to pass along about real estate or how to get rich which we possibly could learn from and adapt to the Christian world view. But, really, as Christians, how much stock can we put in the man who has declared that, "The point is you can't be too greedy." [7]

One of the challenges I face in teaching in Africa is that the people are eager to learn and give Westerners an undue amount of unearned respect. For instance, if they see an American preacher on television they assume he is highly educated and prosperous and therefore what he says must be true. In fact, much of the teaching on television (though certainly not all) is biblically suspect and exploitative, as noted in my earlier discussion of the so-called "Prosperity Gospel."

Discernment Is Proactive

Being discerning is an active, not a passive, activity. We must be in the Word daily and comparing everything we hear against what God says. We must be well-versed to put what we hear in the total context of the Bible. We need to be in Bible study groups where we challenge one another's

---

7   Kunen, James S. *"Pop! Goes the Donald"*, People Magazine, July 9, 1990.

interpretations. We need spiritual guidance by godly pastors and elders. We need to be in prayer that the Holy Spirit will guide us in truth.

We also need to steer clear of the types of empty platitudes we often hear from our politicians and some religious leaders. They are masters at telling us what our "itching ears" want to hear. "For the time will come when men will not put up with sound doctrine. Instead, to suit their own desires, they will gather around them a great number of teachers to say what their itching ears want to hear" (2 Timothy 4:3).

Also, we should be inquisitive. If a politician is promising change, what does that mean? Recently, a friend told me they were supporting a particular candidate because the candidate was for "change." When I asked what kind of change, they could not tell me. Beware. Change can be either good or bad. Don't be lazy. Get the facts behind the claims and measure them up against God's standards.

We need to be careful in who we trust. Sometimes we are impressed by a person's position or status (i.e. the Donald Trump example) and give them instant credibility without measuring their instructions and teachings against the Bible.

I recall one really stupid thing I did out of blind trust. While on a Christmas time ski trip in Jackson Hole, Wyoming my back began having spasms. Desperate, I went to a chiropractor who put me on the table and made some adjustments that seemed to give some partial relief. But then he pointed me to a mini trampoline. Yes, a trampoline! He told me to get on it and jump up and down. Trusting and not thinking, I did what he told me. The result was predictable – I was worse than before. Lesson painfully learned: blind trust is a bad thing.

As Christians and business persons, much of our effectiveness depends upon our teachability tempered with godly discernment.

To continue to grow in the Lord and in wisdom and knowledge for living and business, surround yourself with the people referred to in Psalm 111:10: "The fear of the Lord is the beginning of wisdom; all who follow his precepts have good understanding."

Chapter 7: Teachable

Discussion Questions

1. Discuss the reasons God values a broken spirit (Psalms 51:17).

2. What does it mean to "harden the heart?" How does this compare to a "soft heart?"

3. What are the signs of a leader who is changing from being teachable to being prideful and not teachable?

4. How could becoming unteachable and prideful as a leader be avoided?

5. What consequences have you seen throughout history because the leaders were unteachable and full of pride?

Personal Reflection

1. Do I always have to be right?

2. Am I open to others constructive advice? Do I take things personally rather than try to see God's perspective?

3. Do I always have to be in control? Has this ever caused me to be blind to the reality of a situation?

4. Would God describe me "as a man or woman after God's own heart?"

5. Am I teachable or impressionable?

Chapter 8
Open

"Therefore confess your sins to each other and pray for each other so that you may be healed. The prayer of a righteous man is powerful and effective" (James 5:16).

In the Garden of Eden before the fall of Adam and Eve, there were no sin, shame or secrets.

"The man and his wife were both naked, and they felt no shame" (Genesis 2:25). When Adam and Eve sinned, of course everything changed. Suddenly, they became ashamed and fearful of God and covered themselves.

"Then the eyes of both of them were opened, and they realized they were naked; so they sewed fig leaves together and made coverings for themselves. Then the man and his wife heard the sound of the Lord God as he was walking in the garden in the cool of the day, and they hid from the Lord God among the trees of the garden. But the Lord God called to the man, "Where are you?" He answered, "I heard you in the garden, and I was afraid because I was naked; so I hid."

And he said, "Who told you that you were naked? Have you eaten from the tree that I commanded you not to eat from?" (Genesis 3:7-11).

Too frequently still today people fall into the trap of hiding their sins, mistakes, failures and shortcomings to protect their image. The result is broken fellowship with God and in our other personal relationships.

I am an unabashed free market capitalist, but one of the pitfalls of the western economic system is that it is based upon consumerism. We are not just into consumption of the goods and services we want and need, but also heavily into conspicuous consumption where the primary satisfaction is projecting a successful image to others.

Perception Can Trump Reality

We are more concerned with perception than reality. We are willing to go deep in debt to buy things we don't need so we can convey to others that we are rich. Our contrived "image" becomes the basis of our identity rather than Jesus. This is not confined just to materialism. Some of us get puffed up with Bible knowledge. We want to impress people with our intellect, which gets in the way of our fellowship with the Lord.

I'm sure you also know some name-droppers – the people who diligently try to portray that they are running with the rich and famous.

Image can become everything. I once had a neighbor who was laid off from his job. Rather than telling anyone (including his wife and family), he continued to get up every morning, put on his suit, wait for his car pool ride and get dropped at his former place of employment. He couldn't deal with his fear that others would disrespect him because he lost his job. (Later, he murdered his wife who was leaving him).

Many of us are still hiding behind fig leaves because we cannot deal with the reality of who we are nor do we acknowledge our desperate need for a savior, Jesus.

Have you also noticed that more often than not in political scandals, it is not the crime itself that results in prosecution, but the covering up of the alleged crimes?

In business, it is folly to deny reality and not seek help from trustworthy sources. A real success story of The Rock ministry in Kenya is a man named Paul who runs a sugar cane growing and transport business. Paul wanted to expand his business and presented a very favorable proposal which The Rock was enthusiastic to fund.

Then Paul dropped off the map. We didn't hear from him and did not understand why. When we finally pinned him down, it turned out he had suspended operations because the trailer he used to haul the sugar cane had been reclaimed by a man who had loaned it to him. Because Paul did not disclose to us in the beginning that the trailer was borrowed (Paul did own his own tractor), he feared telling us of his problem. He also did not want to look foolish.

When Paul finally told us his situation, we loaned him the money to buy a trailer and he was back in business. Because of Paul's fig leaf, ten men on his crew were out of work for almost three months, which of course also was a hardship on their families. But once he shared his problem, the men (and Paul) were back in business. The business continues to prosper and grow.

Openness requires humility. Humility makes good business sense because if we cannot share our problems, others can't offer advice or assistance.

Ministry has been a great teacher of humility to me and my wife Margaret. It is my experience that people want to help the ministry, but if they don't know the facts they can't respond. There have been several times when we have been flat broke. In my flesh, I have an instinct to hold back on expressing the true financial struggles for fear people will think we are failing or the ministry is not viable. However, when we present the facts (careful never to "cry wolf") people respond. Without openness, humility and full disclosure of the financial position of The Rock, I don't think the ministry would be around today.

Openness Unleashes Prayer

More important than the fact that openness allows others to encourage and assist us is the power of prayer that openness unleashes.

"Therefore confess your sins to each other and pray for each other so that you may be healed. The prayer of a righteous man is powerful and effective" (James 5:16).

The power of prayer has been amazing in my life. I believe God loves to hear a multitude of intercessory prayer lifted up on behalf of us and our fellow believers. When we hide our needs out of a false sense of pride, we close the door on this type of prayer.

Ministry is a financial challenge. A friend of mine says, "I am a man of faith. You know what faith means? Faith means you're broke!" He uses the example of Elijah and the widow in 1 Kings 17:15. God told a starving Elijah to direct the widow to feed him (along with the woman and her son) her last portion of flour and oil. But as the bowl was emptied daily, God kept filling it up. Missions and ministry is like that. We empty our bowl and are dependent on the Lord to refill it.

I recall about eighteen months after leaving the corporate world for ministry I was about ready to give up because we had been unable to raise any significant financial support. I canceled a trip to Africa for lack of funds, which prompted a group of widows in a small village in Kenya we were scheduled to visit to begin all night prayer sessions on our behalf. We sent out a newsletter detailing our shaky finances and I remember on a Friday praying on my knees, "Lord, I give up. If You want this ministry to survive, You are going to have to do something."

On Saturday morning, a telephone call awoke my wife and me. It was a friend. "Do you still need support for your ministry?" The friend sent a generous check. That night, we went to a Christmas party and someone else handed us a check. Another check came in before the weekend was over and we were able to make the trip to Africa after all and see God do more amazing things.

Two and a half years later, we were broke again. On the last day of training, I asked the men in our first "Doing Business God's Way" class to pray over the ministry's finances. They laid hands on me and prayed with great fervor for financial provision for the ministry in the U.S. The following week, we received a $40,000 donation.

Believe me; these guys' prayers are powerful. Two years later, I asked the men of our second "Doing Business God's Way" class to pray over a friend who assisted in teaching the class whose home had been on the market for almost a year. The friend and his wife had moved to another state and purchased another home so the inability to sell the previous home was a serious hardship. The friend was disappointed that a buyer reneged on an offer earlier during the course.

It turns out that while the men were praying over him that another buyer would buy their home, an offer was being made on the home and shortly after returning from the training, the deal closed.

The Good, The Bad, and The Ugly

Margaret and I believe in sharing the good and bad to those interested in The Rock ministry. When we lived in Africa for a year, we know many people prayed for us daily. We could feel the prayers and will not know fully this side of heaven how God used them to protect us and help us be a blessing to others. When we returned to the U.S. (we now travel three times a year, mobilizing in the U.S. and equipping in Africa) we felt different. Something was missing – we were more easily distracted and discouraged. After a couple of weeks, we realized people had stopped praying for us because we had returned to the U.S. from Africa. We sent out a renewed plea for prayer and our strength and joy in the Lord was renewed.

Margaret and I know that our peace and the fact that we sleep soundly every night is totally irrational from a worldly point of view. In the summer of 2008, I was diagnosed with a serious arthritic condition (praise God it is treatable by expensive medication). Once again we were wondering how we would make our mortgage payment. We felt compelled because of discipleship and reverence issues to leave the church which had embraced our mission work.

In another situation, despite our best efforts at seeking understanding and peacemaking, the leader of another ministry bitterly accused us of betrayal in an unfortunate misunderstanding. Yet our "prayer warriors" were mobilized and we felt the peace of the Lord.

"Do not be anxious about anything, but in everything, by prayer and petition, with thanksgiving, present your requests to God. And the peace of God, which transcends all understanding, will guard your hearts and your minds in Christ Jesus" (Philippians 4:6-7).

A major false belief system that I see holding many believers back from being open and seeking prayer from fellow Christians is that they have the idea that their struggles are personal and that the Creator is too busy with more important things like war and famine. Unfortunately, this also indicates a lack of the intimate personal relationship God desires from his children.

Jesus says: "Are not two sparrows sold for a penny? Yet not one of them will fall to the ground apart from the will of your Father. And even the very hairs of your head are all numbered. So don't be afraid; you are worth more than many sparrows" (Matthew 10:29-31).

The Apostle Paul in his writings mentions a somewhat obscure character named Epaphras. We would all do well to model Epaphras and to pray that the Lord would provide many like Epaphras in our lives.

"Epaphras, who is one of you and a servant of Christ Jesus, sends greetings. He is always wrestling in prayer for you, that you may stand firm in all the will of God, mature and fully assured" (Colossians 4:12).

Wrestle in prayer for others and be open regarding your own struggles so others, like Epaphras, may know how to wrestle in prayer for you.

Oswald Chambers wrote that "prayer is the battle." [8]Enlist your prayer warriors in the battle by being open and disclosing your needs and the forces going against you.

8   Chambers, Oswald. *My Utmost Devotional Bible*. Thomas Nelson Publishing, Nashville, TN: 1992, p. 266

Chapter 8: Open

Discussion Questions

1. Discuss James 5:16. How is openness freeing and healing?

2. Image is many times tied to identity. What do you think God's perspective is on image?

3. How does openness refine us and increase our humility? Give examples.

4. Discuss the effect openness has on prayer.

Personal Reflection

1. What does my "identity in Christ" mean to me?

2. Have I personally experienced healing through openness? Do I need healing now because of a hidden hurt?

3. Is my worldly image to others my idol?

4. Am I embarrassed to share my struggles or ask for prayer?

5. Do I see prayer as a battle?

Chapter 9
Hardworking

"A little sleep, a little slumber, a little folding of the hands to rest – and poverty will come on you like a bandit and scarcity like an armed man" (Proverbs 6:10-11).

Work is a series of paradoxes.

We love our work. We hate our work.

Work is joy. Work is drudgery.

Work sustains us. Work bankrupts us.

Work is invigorating. Work is draining.

Work is identity. Work is meaningless.

Work is affirming. Work is a downer.

Work masters us. Work is mastered by us.

The relationship between a person and his/her work is almost as complex as the romantic relationship between a man and a woman. A whole series of conflicting emotions regarding work can be experienced in a short period of time depending on what kind of day we are having.

The Bible has plenty to say about work. Our attitudes toward our work are closely related to our relationship with God.

God equips us for our work, yet He also has chosen to make it difficult for us. Hard work is a result of Adam's sin in the Garden of Eden. Let's discuss work from a couple of perspectives: why God made it hard and the importance of working hard versus hardly working. Then we can take a look at how to stay on the positive side of the above-mentioned paradoxes.

Legacy of Difficulty

Adam was a guy that had it made in the shade. He worked and tended the garden, but the animals and earth submitted to him. Adam did not have to cultivate crops for food; God just provided them. And then, realizing it was not good for Adam to be alone, God created woman for Adam. One of Adam's big jobs was naming the animals! This was not exactly a stressful existence. Until, that is, Eve was deceived by the serpent and Adam, though not deceived, went along with the rebellion against God by tasting the forbidden fruit.

In doing so, the punishment he brought upon himself from God was that the gig was up when it came to stress-free work.

'To Adam he said, "Because you listened to your wife and ate from the tree about which I commanded you, 'You must not eat of it,' "Cursed is the ground because of you; through painful toil you will eat of it all the days of your life. It will produce thorns and thistles for you, and you will eat the plants of the field. By the sweat of your brow you will eat your food until you return to the ground, since from it you were taken; for dust you are and to dust you will return" (Genesis 3:17-19).

Author and Pastor John McArthur puts it this way:

"Not only is he personally sinful, depraved, fallen, decaying and headed toward death, but he's going to have another problem. He's going to find that the very ground which provides for him his life and sustenance for himself and his family, is not going to willfully submit to him. Life becomes, for him, hard work. The joy of paradise is gone.

"A cursed ground is the opposite then; lack of water, problems with the soil, problems with weeds, problems with the elements, problems with the weather, problems with the destructive animals, problems with destructive birds, problems with destructive organisms and insects. And those are all the problems that plague the ground. The earth will yield enough; it'll yield its bounty. In fact, the earth will yield a rich and wonderful variety for man to enjoy. But in order for that to happen, it's going to take a tremendous effort to get that bounty out of the ground."[9]

---

9   McArthur, John F. Jr. *"The Curse on the Man – Part 1."* 2000.

Does this mean that work is a curse? No, notice that God cursed the ground, not work. The curse is that, through man's own actions, we corrupted a perfect world. It's like Adam's sin polluted a perfect self-sustaining ecosystem. Once dashed, mankind was forced to work hard to sustain life within what became an imperfect and difficult environment. No longer did the earth yield naturally to our needs, all of a sudden man was forced to work it into submission. The curse is that there no longer is a free ride.

We would all do well to acknowledge that work is not designed by God to be easy and that we have a promise from Him that it will be difficult, not only in Genesis but also from Jesus Himself (John 16:33).

Realizing work is designed for trouble helps us anticipate and avoid some problems and be more effective in solving others when they do occur. All businesses have problems. The businesses that anticipate and deal effectively with them succeed; the ones that don't fail.

Working Hard

The Bible references God's low opinion of lazy people.

"For even when we were with you, we gave you this rule: "If a man will not work, he shall not eat" (2 Thessalonians 3:10).

"If anyone does not provide for his relatives, and especially for his immediate family, he has denied the faith and is worse than an unbeliever" (1 Timothy 5:8).

But the faithful hard worker is praised:

"Go to the ant, you sluggard. Consider its ways and be wise! It has no commander, no overseer or ruler, yet it stores its provisions in summer and gathers its food at harvest" (Proverbs 6:6-8).

The ant is praised because it gets the job done without prodding. Unfortunately, lack of supervision and self-discipline can be a pitfall for many. While most successful business owners have the problem of being too driven and working too hard, some who enter business or work independently at a job have problems with putting in a good day's work. There are many opportunities for distractions and diversions that can monopolize the time of undisciplined workers.

One of the greatest examples of hard work, leadership, teamwork, and project management in the Bible is Nehemiah. Devastated by the news that his homeland Jerusalem lay in shambles, he channeled his passion through prayer into a plan approved by the king he served and embraced by his Jewish brethren. Nehemiah pulled off the reconstruction of the wall in Jerusalem by working hard himself, casting a vision, delegating tasks and calling on the Lord's favor.

Motivations for Work

Nehemiah was driven to do the work he did. His passion was to restore to God's people, Israel, their spiritual inheritance by rebuilding the crumbled walls, a symbol of their decline. Money and personal fame were not relevant.

What are your motivations for working? Often, our work becomes the center of our identity instead of Jesus. It has become the thing that defines us and gives us credibility and status with our peers. Typically, when we are asked to introduce ourselves, we automatically give our name and occupation before anything else. A delightful departure from this is the cultural practice among Christians I know in Africa. Here is how they would typically introduce themselves: "My name is John. I am a saved man and I love Jesus. I am the husband of one wife."

I love this type of introduction because it puts the emphasis on where it belongs: our identity in Jesus rather than our job. Of course, it is good to be affirmed in your work. But, the type of affirmation is the key. Do you seek affirmation to feed your ego and increase status or do you seek the affirmation that you are using your God-given talents the best you can to glorify Him?

Solomon saw futility in any work that was not done for God's pleasure.

"So, I hated life because the work that is done under the sun was grievous to me," Solomon said. "All of it is meaningless, a chasing after the wind. I hated all the things I had toiled for under the sun, because I must leave them to the one who comes after me. And who knows whether he will be a wise man or a fool? Yet he will have control over all the work into which I have poured my effort and skill under the sun. This too is meaningless.

"So my heart began to despair over all my toilsome labor under the sun. For a man may do his work with wisdom, knowledge and skill, and then he must leave all he owns to someone who has not worked for it. This too is meaningless and a great misfortune. What does a man get for all the toil and anxious striving with which he labors under the sun? All his days his work is pain and grief; even at night his mind does not rest. This too is meaningless.

"A man can do nothing better than to eat and drink and find satisfaction in his work. This too, I see, is from the hand of God, for without him, who can eat or find enjoyment? To the man who pleases him, God gives wisdom, knowledge and happiness, but to the sinner he gives the task of gathering and storing up wealth to hand it over to the one who pleases God. This too is meaningless, a chasing after the wind" (Ecclesiastes 2:17-26).

We all are prone to "chasing after the wind" – seeking peace and satisfaction in personal achievements and success in our work.

Is Balance Biblical?

It has become somewhat of a cliché that we must seek "balance" in our lives among work, play, family and faith. This concept of balance has a common sense flare to it and it might be useful to the extent that it discourages us from overlooking all in favor of work. However, I can find no Biblical basis for the concept of balance. On the contrary, we are called to tilt the scales totally toward God. This is what was demanded of the rich young ruler (Matthew 19:16-23).

There also is the difficult story of the person who was instructed not to delay joining Jesus by attending his father's funeral (Matthew 8:21-22).

Each of the disciples was expected immediately to leave family and jobs behind to follow Jesus.

Of course, the greatest commandment is to love the Lord "with all your heart and with all your soul and with all your mind" (Matthew 22:37).

"For in him we live and move and have our being" (Acts 17:28).

Where is the balance in those verses?

The point is we must depend on God alone to set our priorities for us. This is frightening to many of us because it calls for total surrender and total faith. There are no human formulas to guide us. There is only God. We are expected to discern our Maker's will not only for our lives, but for each moment of each day. To me, true fulfillment is knowing I am doing exactly what God would have me do at this precise moment.

Previously, I had fallen for the world's definition of success defined in monetary terms. We compete with one another to distinguish ourselves with our incomes and wealth. Business owners take temporary pleasure in the battle with other companies over profits and performance. And the very wealthy often compete with themselves. Profits and wealth become a scorecard and there is a never-ending quest for more money and no amount ultimately satisfies.

"Whoever loves money never has money enough; whoever loves wealth is never satisfied with his income. This too is meaningless" (Ecclesiastes 5:10).

Let God Direct Your Steps

"I know, O Lord, that a man's life is not his own; it is not for man to direct his steps" (Jeremiah 10:23).

Sometimes God directs us to do things that, quite frankly, we might think are nuts. For me, leaving the corporate world and entering the international mission field was not a rational decision that deferred to any concept of balance. It simply was what God called me to do.

I remember when I shared with my wife that the Lord was calling me into full-time faith missions, she replied, "Well, Honey, that's great for you and I will pray for you. But I have no desire to go into missions."

For many nights after the decision was made, we lay awake in bed staring at the ceiling fretting over our financial future as I was off to a very slow start raising personal support to do the mission work. Many times I questioned whether I had correctly discerned God's will, but always He opened and closed doors to keep me in missions. Only after I finally literally got down on my knees with my wife and prayed, "Lord, if you want this ministry to succeed you are going to have to do something," did things turn around. My total surrender to His plan and His power was the victory and the breakthrough.

Since then, the Lord also brought my wife Margaret into the mission work and given her an even greater zeal than me. Our lives are totally out of balance but we believe they are in God's will at the same time.

Tragic results happen when we forge ahead despite His "Not now" answer. (God always answers prayer – either "Yes," "No," or "Not now"). Equally destructive is when we fail to respond when He does say "Now." I know men and women who are called to full-time ministry work, but are holding back until they can earn enough money to make the change from business to ministry painlessly. They are conflicted and torn because they do not believe that where God truly provides a vision, He also provides a provision.

God provides seasons in our lives (Ecclesiastes 3:1-8). He may put a passion in our heart at a young age but not bring it to fruition until much later in life. We have to discern not only His will, but also His timing. Sometimes we may be impatient with Him as He says, "Not now." Other times we may be terrified when He says, "Now!" Only through a close relationship with the Lord can we hear His guidance and trust Him to accomplish His purpose in our lives.

Recently my friend Cliff, 67, joined our ministry. He developed a passion for missions while listening to Moody Bible Institute radio programs as a boy growing up in Illinois. As a young man in college, he studied social work with an emphasis in world missions, although he left school one term short of getting a degree. After a lifelong business career, Cliff at age 66 completed his degree requirements and was awarded his diploma. Although he has been active in church lay mission work for many years, the Lord finally blessed Cliff by allowing him to fulfill his lifelong passion of full-time mission service. Cliff's season has come.

Is Retirement Biblical?

Cliff is a great example of someone who has no desire to be retired in the traditional sense of the word. He is on the front lines for the Lord applying a lifetime of knowledge and experience for the Kingdom. Where did our culture come up with this preoccupation with retirement?

I have a friend who retired and, when people would ask him what he did, he would reply jokingly, "I'm a piddler." What a waste!

Where is the biblical justification for working all your life so you can move to Florida and play golf all day year-round?

Also, where is the biblical justification for spending a lifetime storing up treasures for our old age?

Don't get me wrong – I am all for wise and prudent financial planning to make sure our needs can be met when we no longer can be income earners. It just seems to me the emphasis has gotten a little out of whack and our concern for the future (which is not guaranteed – we could die tomorrow) sometimes causes us to resist God's call to us in the present.

You Are a Minister

Finally, I embrace the teaching that as Christians, we all are called to be ministers, though certainly not always in the vocational sense.

If you are a business owner, you are God's minister disguised in a broken world as a business owner. If you are a teacher, you are God's minister disguised in a broken world as a teacher. If you are a sales person, you are God's minister disguised in a broken world as a sales person. God is your boss and He has blessed you with a job and income to provide for your needs. Show your gratitude and love for Him by shining your light for Him in whatever work you do. Work hard, do good and share the Gospel by your example, using words when necessary.

Chapter 9: Hardworking

Discussion Questions

1. Discuss the paradoxes of work and how you cope with them.

2. How have you seen others' attitudes about work impact your work environment?

3. What does the Bible teach about consequences and obedience? Discuss having a balanced life in relationship to what it says in Jeremiah 10:23. What is the difference between having balance and boundaries? How do setting boundaries honor the Lord when you reflect on what the Bible says about "letting our yes be yes and no be no."

4. What examples can you give about God using you at work to impact others?

Personal Reflection

1. What is my prime motivation for work?

2. What honors God most about my work?

3. Do I leave God at home when I go to work?

4. Am I aware of His presence in every situation?

5. How often do I pray for specific direction by God in my work related decisions?

Chapter 10
Diligent

"Whatever you do, work at it with all your heart, as working for the Lord, not for men, since you know that you will receive an inheritance from the Lord as a reward. It is the Lord Christ you are serving" (Colossians 3:23-24).

When you are running your business or doing your job "as working for the Lord," things change. There is a new standard and a new desire to excel – not just for yourself or your company, but first and foremost for God.

Going through the motions without the passion is not enough anymore. Shortcuts are unacceptable. Moral compromises are out of the question when "it is the Lord Jesus Christ you are serving."

Working with excellence means being diligent in all you do. Diligence is a primary attribute that Paul encouraged for his understudy, Timothy. Diligence was seen by Paul as a way to set a godly example and impact others.

"Command and teach these things," Paul told Timothy. "Don't let anyone look down on you because you are young, but set an example for the believers in speech, in life, in love, in faith and in purity. Until I come, devote yourself to the public reading of Scripture, to preaching and to teaching. Do not neglect your gift, which was given you through a prophetic message when the body of elders laid their hands on you.

"Be diligent in these matters; give yourself wholly to them, so that everyone may see your progress. Watch your life and doctrine closely. Persevere in them, because if you do, you will save both yourself and your hearers" (1 Timothy 4:11-16).

Proverbs has much to say about diligence as well:

"Lazy hands make a man poor, but diligent hands bring wealth" (Proverbs 10:4).

"Diligent hands will rule, but laziness ends in slave labor" (Proverbs 12:24).

"The lazy man does not roast his game, but the diligent man prizes his possessions" (Proverbs 12:27).

"The sluggard craves and gets nothing, but the desires of the diligent are fully satisfied" (Proverbs 13:4).

"The plans of the diligent lead to profit, as surely as haste leads to poverty" (Proverbs 21:5).

Haste is an appropriate opposite of diligence, as is sloppiness. When you are working for the Lord, just getting the job done is not enough. We desire to get it done efficiently and excellently. Our desire is not only to work hard for the Lord, but to work smart for the Lord as well to maximize the return on the talents He has given us.

Good vs. Excellent

The notion that good can be the enemy of excellence takes root in our hearts. We beware of ruts, routines and comfort in our work or business. We're always looking for a way to improve our work to honor the Lord.

As Jesus followers, we are called upon to be "living sacrifices."

"Therefore, I urge you, brothers, in view of God's mercy, to offer your bodies as living sacrifices, holy and pleasing to God – this is your spiritual act of worship. Do not conform any longer to the pattern of this world, but be transformed by the renewing of your mind. Then you will be able to test and approve what God's will is – his good, pleasing and perfect will" (Romans 12:1-2).

Because our business or work is a large part of our life, we should consider it as part of the sacrifice to the Lord which He wants as our "spiritual act of worship." And we know that God desires only that we surrender our best to Him.

"When you bring injured, crippled or diseased animals and offer them as sacrifices, should I accept them from your hands?" says the Lord. "Cursed is the cheat who has an acceptable male in his flock and vows to give it, but then sacrifices a blemished animal to the Lord. For I am a great king," says the Lord Almighty, "and my name is to be feared among the nations" (Malachi 1:13-14).

In other words, if you are offering anything less than the best you have to God in your business or work, you are slighting Him. God seeks diligence and the best you have to offer in His strength.

A good example of giving your best is my friend mentioned in Chapter 4, who despite a dominant market share and 99 percent customer satisfaction rating pressed ahead to increase his company's customer rating on value for services received.

It is easy to lower our standards and forget that everything we do is to be as if unto the Lord. A tough coach or teacher can bring out the best in us. Competition can drive us to new levels of achievement. Courtship can bring out our best. Being in the public spotlight forces us to put our best foot forward.

I remember being in Uganda during the run up to the Commonwealth Heads of Government Meeting (CHOGM) hosted in 2007 by that country and attended by the Queen of England.

Everyone in the former British colony was excited that "the queen is coming." Roads were rebuilt, beautification projects were undertaken, luxury hotels were constructed, the airport at Entebbe got a face lift and streets and communities were cleaned and cleared of rubbish. This was all very impressive, but the thought that came to mind was why can't people be as excited about the King who is coming, Jesus Christ? Should not we live to honor Him more than the queen?

"No one knows about that day or hour, not even the angels in heaven, nor the Son, but only the Father. As it was in the days of Noah, so it will be at the coming of the Son of Man. For in the days before the flood, people were eating and drinking, marrying and giving in marriage, up to the day Noah entered the ark; and they knew nothing about what would happen until the flood came and took them all away. That is how it will be at the coming of the Son of Man. Two men will be in the field; one will be taken and the other left. Two women will be grinding with a hand mill; one will be taken and the other left.

"Therefore keep watch, because you do not know on what day your Lord will come" (Matthew 24:36-42).

The King is coming! "Behold, I am coming soon!" (Revelation 22:7). Are you ready to present Him your very best?

Chapter 10: Diligent

Discussion Questions

1. Do you believe what it says in Colossians 3:23-24?

2. Have you seen this in action around you?

3. Discuss how this might impact the way people work if it was widely implemented.

4. How does diligence and excellence impact others when leaders exhibit these characteristics?

5. Give examples of these kinds of leaders and what you have learned from them.

Personal Reflection

1. Am I satisfied with my personal performance?

2. If not what am I going to do differently?

3. Reflect on successes because I have been diligent.

4. Does my work show excellence and that I am giving my best to the Lord?

5. Re-read the verses in Proverbs and think about how they apply personally.

Chapter 11
Providers for Our Families

"If anyone does not provide for his relatives, and especially for his immediate family, he has denied the faith and is worse than an unbeliever" (1 Timothy 5:8).

God is a God of order. He has placed us in families and given us specific roles and responsibilities within those families.

Our Family Roles

As stated in Ephesians 5:22-29:

"Wives, submit to your husbands as to the Lord. For the husband is the head of the wife as Christ is the head of the church, his body, of which he is the Savior. Now as the church submits to Christ, so also wives should submit to their husbands in everything. Husbands, love your wives, just as Christ loved the church and gave himself up for her to make her holy, cleansing her by the washing with water through the word, and to present her to himself as a radiant church, without stain or wrinkle or any other blemish, but holy and blameless. In this same way, husbands ought to love their wives as their own bodies. He who loves his wife loves himself. After all, no one ever hated his own body, but he feeds and cares for it, just as Christ does the church– for we are members of his body."

Men are to love and care for their wives sacrificially, even to the point of death as with the comparison of Jesus dying on the cross for us. Men who love their wives in this way most likely will find that women will respond gratefully to their God-ordained headship in the family.

God's Design of Men and Women

Genesis teaches us God's design for men and women. His judgment on Eve was that she would have pain in child bearing and "your desire will be for your husband, and he will rule over you" (Genesis 3:16). Woman is relational; her desire is for her husband.

God's judgment for Adam was that his work would become difficult and "by the sweat of your brow you will eat your food" (Genesis 3:19). So, while woman was given a relational disposition, man was given a task-oriented disposition. Can't you see these differences as an underlying theme in relational difficulties between the sexes? Women want to be heard and understood. Men just want to get on with the task at hand. Women desire love and affection; men want respect and acknowledgement of the tasks they have achieved.

Women are nurturers; men are doers. The way God wired the sexes seems to lend itself best to the woman caring for the "nest" – children and home – while the man provides for the home. However, there are no scriptural commands to that effect and there is freedom in this area. Note that women are not told to submit to men in general – just to their husbands. So there is nothing to hold them back in the workplace.

Once again, motivation is the key in determining who does or does not earn income outside the home in your own family.

A Lesson Learned the Hard Way

My wife and I have strong regrets in this area. We attended university in the 1970s and bought the lie of women's lib – that there is no difference between men and women except plumbing. My wife Margaret, as an undiscipled baby believer at the time – felt a strong need to establish her identity and credibility professionally. I was all for that as I saw it as taking the heat off of me to be the sole provider. (This was before I gave my life to Jesus).

At one point when I transferred jobs, she mentioned maybe she would like to be a stay-home mom with our pre-school daughter Audrey. I discouraged her, telling her she would be bored out of her skull staying home. I suppose I partially believed that, but truth be known I also wanted the income she could bring home.

As the years went by, I saw the bad consequences of my advice. My wife was stressed at work, we accumulated more things which required more income to make the payments and my daughter Audrey did not receive the main thing she needed – our time. I have been told that children spell love T-I-M-E. We did not give her enough of it and I'm sure that led to some acting out for attention and bad behavior in her teen years.

If we had it to do over again, my wife would have stayed home at least until Audrey graduated from high school. I'm sure we could have managed on my income had we made that a priority.

Many young couples today continue to fall into a financial trap. After they are married, they both work to achieve the lifestyle they desire before having children. The problem often is that by the time they have their first child they have accumulated a mortgage, car payments and credit card debt that preclude the wife's option of staying home without a separate income.

My advice from hard experience is put family over career and make sure one parent is always there for your children. The love, nurturing and spiritual guidance only possible by a parent's time for a child is, I believe, part of the biblical command to provide for your immediate family.

Whatever It Takes

God has made providing for our families a command, not an option. In other words, whatever honest work it takes to provide the basic needs of your family is required.

This "whatever it takes" attitude may sometimes cause us to humble ourselves and do work that we might consider in our flesh to be beneath us. The chairman of our mission organization The Rock, Dan Vick, tells a story of hardship when he was building his business which later boomed and was sold.

During a particularly rough time in the start-up period, he and his wife Angie cleaned homes for others to make ends meet. That is the type of commitment and humility that God honors.

"For whoever exalts himself will be humbled, and whoever humbles himself will be exalted" (Matthew 23:12).

In lean times for our nonprofit organization, we have worked a concession stand at Dallas Cowboys football games. It is great to get executives and students alike to join with us and do good, honest, hard labor for the Lord.

It sure beats buying a lottery ticket – which is illustrative of what many people do in times of trouble. They are looking for a bolt of lightning to solve their problems. Yes, God can do miracles, but often He is putting us through a process with no shortcuts allowed.

Risk Taking

Gambling is not the only risk taking that can negatively affect our ability to provide for our families. In evaluating our business, personal investments or commitments, we must always determine if failure of the venture or investment would prevent us from performing our biblical mandate to support our family. "Due diligence" is required on our part to protect our families.

Creative problem solving to provide for our families does not have to be risky. I know several pastors in Africa who are industrious to support their families because their poor congregations cannot provide the basic needs of the pastor and his family. These pastors raise pigs and chickens or grow crops to feed their families and produce income.

On the other hand, I know other pastors who refuse to do such work and instead pray and wait upon some benevolent person to give them money. Some even test God. For instance, it is not unusual for an African pastor to have a school fee sponsorship program for children in their church. Some pastors will take the donated money and give it to any children but their own. Their belief is that God will see them sacrificing their own children's education for others and that somehow God will bless this sacrifice. I see this as testing God and denying His mandate to us to provide for our families.

Conversely, I know of another African church where leaders have plowed through Christmas gifts meant for sponsored children to claim the best items for their own children before passing them on to the intended recipients. Of course, this is abominable to God and has nothing to do with providing for our own families in a godly way.

Creating Your Legacy

It is an American dream that each generation provides for a better future for its children. This is a noble goal, but often the emphasis is misplaced on monetary and material gain. The best and most enduring legacy you can leave is a life lived as a devoted follower of Jesus.

Unfortunately, too often the most destructive inheritance you can leave is money. Most of us probably know "trust babies" whose inheritances have turned them into undisciplined, unappreciative hedonists who don't know the value of hard work. Or the result could be like the prodigal son who asked for and received his inheritance early.

"Jesus continued: "There was a man who had two sons. The younger one said to his father, 'Father, give me my share of the estate.' So he divided his property between them.

"Not long after that, the younger son got together all he had, set off for a distant country and there squandered his wealth in wild living. After he had spent everything, there was a severe famine in that whole country, and he began to be in need" (Luke 15:11-14).

In this story, the young man was able to return to his father and receive grace, forgiveness and restoration because the inheritance was given early. Unfortunately, that is not always the case today with people whose lives are destroyed by inherited wealth.

It is biblical to leave an inheritance (Proverbs 13:22). But we need to make sure the physical inheritance we leave behind does not get in the way of the spiritual inheritance of our offspring, which is life forever with God in heaven (1 Peter 1:3-4).

One of my well-to-do friends with two daughters already has informed them not to count on a big inheritance. He plans to give most of his money to Kingdom work and leave a small amount for his children. This motivates the daughters to develop their God-given abilities to the maximum in the knowledge that they don't "have it made" due to their father's success.

Another friend has started to teach his adult children on the value of giving. The friend provides annual designated gifts to each of his offspring with the provision that they give it all away to Kingdom-worthy causes of their choice.

These actions keep in proper perspective the worldly and heavenly inheritances we are to receive as believers in Jesus.

"The Spirit himself testifies with our spirit that we are God's children. Now if we are children, then we are heirs – heirs of God and co-heirs with Christ, if indeed we share in his sufferings in order that we may also share in his glory" (Romans 8:16-17).

Chapter 11: Providing for Our Families

Discussion Questions

1. Explore God's roles in the family versus the world's perspective.

2. How does the provision for the family impact the dynamics of male and female relationships?

3. God values men and women equally however He has made them different. Discuss how this truth has been challenging between men and women.

4. There is freedom spiritually in how each family handles the issue of provision. Discuss what you have seen work and not work based on different phases of the life cycle.

5. Discuss risk taking, financial planning and your experience in planning for your family.

Personal Reflection

1. How am I providing for my family? Am I doing whatever it takes even if I have to humble myself to do menial work?

2. Is there unity and order in my family that honors God?

3. What areas of my financial planning am I happy about and what things would I change?

4. Are my family members participating in providing for the family? What skills are they learning?

5. What legacy am I leaving for others (spiritual, financial, and emotional)?

Chapter 12
Conscientious Stewards

"His master replied, 'Well done, good and faithful servant! You have been faithful with a few things; I will put you in charge of many things. Come and share your master's happiness!'" (Matthew 25:21).

God entrusts us with many things, including our very lives and every breath we take. How we manage and care for the gifts He has provided is the measure of our stewardship.

We are stewards of our planet; we are stewards of our possessions; we are stewards of our faith; we are stewards of our relationships; we are stewards of our time and, most of all, our very lives.

A Matter of Attitude

Stewardship is first an attitude before it is an action. It is a measure of our thankfulness for what God has provided. Stewardship is an attitude of gratitude. Lack of stewardship, or neglectfulness toward what God has provided us, shows a lack of respect, disdain and even a despising of the gifts we have received.

In the previous chapter, we discussed the prodigal son and his disregard for his inheritance. His lack of stewardship led to disastrous results. Esau in the Bible was another person who despised his birthright, giving it up to his brother Jacob for some bread and a bowl of stew.

Esau's disregard for his inheritance and God's reaction to it are evident in the Book of Hebrews: "See that no one is sexually immoral, or is godless like Esau, who for a single meal sold his inheritance rights as the oldest son. Afterward, as you know, when he wanted to inherit this blessing, he was rejected. He could bring about no change of mind, though he sought the blessing with tears" (Hebrews 12:16-17).

Ugly Consequences of Poor Stewardship

Being a poor steward has dire consequences. Another servant from the parable referenced in Matthew Chapter 25 at the beginning of this chapter who did not produce a return on what was given him was severely chastised.

"His master replied, 'You wicked, lazy servant! So you knew that I harvest where I have not sown and gather where I have not scattered seed? Well then, you should have put my money on deposit with the bankers, so that when I returned I would have received it back with interest."

"'Take the talent from him and give it to the one who has the ten talents. For everyone who has will be given more, and he will have an abundance. Whoever does not have, even what he has will be taken from him. And throw that worthless servant outside, into the darkness, where there will be weeping and gnashing of teeth'" (Matthew 25:26-30).

I have witnessed sad examples of poor stewardship in Africa. One ministry pleaded for tillers and tractors to cultivate crops. However, when they were provided the equipment, it was left in the field to rust and be pilfered. When one of the donors of the equipment offered to pay for repairs so the equipment could be loaned for a short period to another ministry to grow food, the ministry refused – choosing instead to let the equipment sit useless rather than share it. This represented not only poor stewardship and a void of generosity, but also a lack of understanding that God owns all things.

Stewardship also involves wisdom in protecting what God has provided. Hezekiah was a poor example of this. So enamored of his kingly possessions that he had to show them off, he allowed representatives of the rival king of Babylon to see his treasures. "There is nothing among my treasures that I did not show them" (2 Kings 20:15). The Prophet Isaiah then informed him: "The time will surely come when everything in your palace, and all that your fathers have stored up until this day, will be carried off to Babylon. Nothing will be left, says the Lord" (2 Kings 20:17).

Judas was another poor steward. He was put in charge of the disciples' money, only to show himself to be a thief.

Positive Role Models

Of course, there also are many examples of excellent stewardship. Joseph the son of Jacob modeled excellence in managing all his affairs and resources, including all the bounty of Egypt. His wise management saved his family and many others from starvation during a time of famine.

Nehemiah made excellent use of resources in rebuilding Jerusalem's wall. Job was said to be a man of great wealth and uprightness. "There is no one on earth like him; he is blameless and upright, a man who fears God and shuns evil" (Job 1:8).

In our daily lives, we should be thankful, blameless and upright in tending to all the blessings God has provided us. A clean, orderly, well-maintained, organized business reflects well on the business. It inspires confidence, excellence and good stewardship. A dirty, messy, ill-maintained, disorganized business reflects poorly on the business. It does not inspire confidence in the business' ability to perform, its pursuit of excellence, nor its concept of stewardship. The same can be said for our homes and selves.

A primary point of stewardship goes way beyond maintaining what we have been given, but also into multiplying it for the Kingdom. This is the point of the story of the talents. God is into multiplication, not just mere addition. This applies to the resources He gives us and the spiritual impact He wants us to have on others as well.

Stewarding Your Time

One of the greatest gifts we have on this earth is time. We talk about "spending" time or "investing" time. It is a precious asset. Are you a good steward of your time? Being a good steward of your time means focusing on things that matter. Relaxation, renewal and refreshment matter, so those certainly are godly uses of time.

But excesses in downtime, play or work do not represent godly stewardship of our time. Endless hours of mindless television viewing represent poor stewardship of one of your most precious assets.

Sometimes resistance to change can hinder our stewardship. To be the best steward of our time and resources, we need to embrace new ideas and technology that can increase our efficiency and effectiveness. We are called not only to work hard, but to work smart as well.

Giving

Another indispensable element in stewardship is giving to the Kingdom. That is the subject of the next chapter.

"Honor the Lord with your wealth, with the first fruits of all your crops; then your barns will be filled to overflowing, and your vats will brim over with new wine" (Proverbs 3:9-10).

Chapter 12: Conscientious Steward

Discussion Questions

1. Describe experiences where God has given you "a few things" to be in charge of and has multiplied them because of faithfulness.

2. How does stewardship reflect the "condition of the heart"? Give examples.

3. In Hebrews 12:16-17 consequences and "the condition of the heart" is revealed. What examples in today's society are the same?

4. What are some current day "ugly consequences" of poor stewardship?

5. Discuss some of the good stewards in the Bible like Joseph and Nehemiah and their rewards.

Personal Reflection

1. Does my life reflect good stewardship with my body, business and home life?

2. Am I spending my time wisely each day?

3. What time stewardship issues do I need to work on in my life?

4. Are my stewardship priorities in line with God's Biblical priorities?

5. How does my leadership in the area of stewardship impact those around me?

Chapter 13
Generous in Our Offerings

"Each man should give what he has decided in his heart to give, not reluctantly or under compulsion, for God loves a cheerful giver" (2 Corinthians 9:7).

Have you noticed every attribute of a godly person takes us right back to Chapter 1, "What Is the Condition of Your Heart?"

God does not want you to give for any other reason than an expression of the love and obedience in your heart for Him and His work. Jesus has harsh things to say about those who give with impure hearts.

"Woe to you, teachers of the law and Pharisees, you hypocrites! You give a tenth of your spices – mint, dill and cumin. But you have neglected the more important matters of the law – justice, mercy and faithfulness. You should have practiced the latter, without neglecting the former. You blind guides! You strain out a gnat but swallow a camel" (Matthew 23:23-24).

And, without love, giving is worthless to the giver: "If I give all I possess to the poor and surrender my body to the flames, but have not love, I gain nothing" (1 Corinthians 13:3).

Giving is a spiritual gift ("those able to help others" 1 Corinthians 12:28), but it also is a spiritual discipline. It's kind of like working out. You want to do it, you know you should do it and you know you will feel better after you do it, but you need the discipline to do it in the first place.

Perhaps that is why God has told us to give our "first fruits" (Exodus 23:19) to Him. It not only is an acknowledgement that everything belongs to Him (Psalm 24:1; 1 Corinthians 10:26) and is a gift from Him, but also that He is #1 on our priority list. "For where your treasure is, there your heart will be also" (Matthew 6:21).

More Than Money

Giving is not only financial. We can offer our time and our talents for the Lord's service as well. Writing a check is good. But writing a check along with comforting others, toiling for the Lord and/or offering our skills is better.

The ability and discipline to honor God by giving to His Kingdom should be the greatest satisfaction in your business or vocation. From a strictly secular viewpoint, the objective for any business is to make a profit. As long as the profit is made in a way that honors God, this is necessary and noble. But if that is the sole objective, ultimately the endeavor is futile. The overriding objective should be to profit the Kingdom of God.

"What good will it be for a man if he gains the whole world, yet forfeits his soul?" (Matthew 16:26).

In The Rock business incubation/development program, we differentiate between our inputs, our desired outputs (short term) and our desired outcomes (long term).

Our inputs are the resources (human, financial, spiritual and Bible teaching) that we supply to potential godly leaders with a background and desire to start or grow a business. Our desired outputs are profitable companies led by disciples of Jesus Christ. Our desired outcomes are that the businessman's influence as a disciple is a light for Jesus that strengthens family, church, community and ultimately the nation.

In Africa, we are looking for more and stronger churches; families able to disciple, provide for and educate their children; and strong Christian leaders to emerge from The Rock business program who will fill influential positions in the social and political structure. Ultimately we believe the Lord will work through these leaders to reduce corruption and witchcraft in these countries – powerful strongholds that are a stench to God and obstacles to eradicating widespread poverty.

If all The Rock accomplishes is the output of creating profitable businesses by people who call themselves Christians, we will have failed. God has a greater purpose for these businesses.

What is your vision? How can you use your company or your career to advance the Kingdom and bring glory to God? If you are focused only on profit margins and net earnings, you are missing out on a great adventure of being a part of God's army.

You Cannot Out Give God

I have made clear already my repulsion to the so-called "Prosperity Gospel" (See Introduction – Rich Toward God).

We do not give to get. Having said that ... I also have found in my personal experience that, when led by the Spirit and when done with pure motives, it is impossible to out give God. I would like to share a personal example.

Early in my missionary career, I got to know an African pastor who was attending a Bible college in the U.S. His wife stayed behind in Kenya to manage their small church in the bush of Kenya while he was being trained. The pastor shared the great need in his Kenyan village for a mercy home for children due to the number of kids orphaned by AIDS.

When I planned my first trip to Africa, the pastor pleaded with me to visit his village and be hosted by his wife. I agreed and all the villagers were very excited about the upcoming visit. They also anticipated that I would be the answer they were looking for to build the orphanage in their village. (Most Africans assume all Westerners are rich and able to meet their needs if only we will do so. Unfortunately, I was broke at the time).

Before I arrived, the widows of the village were holding all night prayer sessions for my visit and the hope I would be able to help them with the children's home.

I was dropped off public transport a few miles from the village, where many villagers met me with singing, signs, flowers and branches attached to bicycles. I rode the back of a bicycle on the dirt road to the village. As we neared, the children joined the caravan and led the way with beautiful singing.

During the brief visit, I was touched by the need of the children and the way the widows in the village had banded together to take care of them the best they could. I preached and was amazed that some people walked for two days to attend the services.

When I left, I told the pastor's wife I would trust the Lord to use me to help provide them with a home for the children. God touched my heart and I was burdened by the need.

Months passed and the widows of the village continued all night prayer vigils asking the Lord to provide the home through me. I must tell you, I could feel the prayers and I cried out myself to the Lord to show me the way. As much as I told people of the need, no one responded.

A year later, I returned to the village empty-handed, this time accompanied by my wife Margaret. We were welcomed warmly again. The pastor had told me the people in his village, particularly the men, were losing heart and needed encouragement so I prepared a sermon on perseverance. But, as I prayed with my wife before the service, I felt a clear leading from the Lord to preach instead on giving. I was concerned that the church did not take up an offering in their services, the justification given that they could not be expected to give when they were so poor. However, I had seen in other impoverished churches how the people were blessed by even giving a handful of rice or an egg as an offering.

Teaching Giving to Those Who Have Nothing

So I threw out my prepared sermon and taught on giving. I told the story of Elijah and the widow (1 Kings 17:7-16). As Elijah was starving during a drought he came upon a widow and her son. He asked for food from them, even though they had "only a handful of flour in a jar and a little oil in a jug." The widow said she and her son were preparing to eat the final portion and die.

"Elijah said to her, "Don't be afraid. Go home and do as you have said. But first make a small cake of bread for me from what you have and bring it to me, and then make something for yourself and your son. For this is what the Lord, the God of Israel, says: 'The jar of flour will not be used up and the jug of oil will not run dry until the day the Lord gives rain on the land.'"

"She went away and did as Elijah had told her. So there was food every day for Elijah and for the woman and her family. For the jar of flour was not used up and the jug of oil did not run dry, in keeping with the word of the Lord spoken by Elijah" (1 Kings 17:13-16).

I had their attention. I continued on with Jesus' story of the widow's sacrificial offering:

"Jesus sat down opposite the place where the offerings were put and watched the crowd putting their money into the temple treasury. Many rich people threw in large amounts. But a poor widow came and put in two very small copper coins, worth only a fraction of a penny. Calling his disciples to him, Jesus said, "I tell you the truth, this poor widow has put more into the treasury than all the others. They all gave out of their wealth; but she, out of her poverty, put in everything – all she had to live on" (Mark 12:31-43).

I moved on to Malachi 3:10: "Bring the whole tithe into the storehouse, that there may be food in my house. Test me in this," says the Lord Almighty, "and see if I will not throw open the floodgates of heaven and pour out so much blessing that you will not have room enough for it."

I concluded with a true story very close to home for the villagers. It had been told to me by a member of another mission organization, Engineering Ministries International. The team agreed to visit the village for several days to draft plans for a home for children and a church building should funding become available.

The services of EMI are free, but so the recipients will have a stake in the project, they ask the hosts to feed and house them during their stay. The pastor's wife made the plea in church for help in hosting the guests, but only one widow responded. She gave the equivalent of a U.S. dime – a gift similar to the one made the by widow praised by Jesus.

No one on the EMI team knew at the time of their visit to the village that this woman gave, nor that she was the only one who gave. (The pastor's wife struggled and put together the arrangements herself).

The giving widow also was crippled. She lived in a crumbing earthen home but still managed to take in and care for some orphaned children. The engineers saw her heart for the Lord and love for the children despite her disability and poverty. They were touched and agreed to pool their resources and build her a new house! So they did! Not just a house – but the finest one in the whole village!

Only after the visit did the engineers learn the widow was the only one who gave for their provision. As I said before, it is impossible to out give God!

This story, which amazingly was unknown to the villagers prior to my sermon, really lifted the spirits of those attending the service. It ignited a spirit-filled time of celebration, singing and dancing. It was amazing. Then the pastor called for an offering. People lined up during the singing to give small coins, small bills and even a large bag of rice. Joyful giving it was.

The thrill of the moment was tempered when the pastor, who had returned from Bible college to his village, announced the offerings were to be given to me. My instincts cried out inside me, "No, this is not for me! This is your offering to the Lord in your own community of believers!" But to decline the gift would be considered a rude offense. I humbly accepted the offering, which totaled the equivalent of about $20 U.S., and trusted the Lord to tell me what to do with it. They kept the rice for the pastor's family.

From Giving from Lack to Giving From Abundance

On the flight back to the U.S. with my bag full of coins, God gave me an idea. Why not tell the story of this amazing act of giving to my friends in the U.S. and ask them to purchase a coin as a way to raise money for the children's home the village needed so desperately?

My wife Margaret helped expand on the idea – we could polish the coins and sell them as necklaces and bracelets and even use the smaller ones for earrings. Well, the idea took off and people responded immediately. We charged $20 per shilling (a shilling equals about one and half cents U.S.). We raised enough to build the home and returned months later for its grand opening.

I recall at the service before the opening, the pastor and church had taken God's message on giving to heart: They took up two offerings during the service!

Chapter 13: Generous in Our Offerings

Discussion Questions

1. Discuss the "condition of the heart" in relation to giving.

2. Why is it dangerous to expect specific results from God when we give?

3. What does God say about giving in 2 Corinthians 9:7?

4. Who is the owner of everything? How can we show our appreciation?

5. Read Matthew 6:21 and explain what it means in the area of practical application.

6. What does the statement "you can't out give God" mean? Discuss the implications of Malachi 3:10.

Personal Reflection

1. What is my perspective on honoring God by giving?

2. Do I believe God owns and provides everything we need but not everything we want?

3. If I lost everything I own today would I be angry at God? Why?

4. What am I going to do differently after studying about giving?

5. When I gave sacrificially in a spontaneous way because I felt I needed to do it out of obedience to the Lord how did I feel? Did God respond in unexpected ways following this obedience?

Chapter 14
Involved in the Life of Your Church

"Now you are the body of Christ, and each one of you is a part of it" (1 Corinthians 12:27).

As a godly business person or worker in the Kingdom, you are not designed to go it alone. You need the body of Christ (the church) and the body of Christ needs you!

"Now the body is not made up of one part but of many. If the foot should say, "Because I am not a hand, I do not belong to the body," it would not for that reason cease to be part of the body. And if the ear should say, "Because I am not an eye, I do not belong to the body," it would not for that reason cease to be part of the body. If the whole body were an eye, where would the sense of hearing be? If the whole body were an ear, where would the sense of smell be? But in fact God has arranged the parts in the body, every one of them, just as he wanted them to be. If they were all one part, where would the body be? As it is, there are many parts, but one body.

"The eye cannot say to the hand, 'I don't need you!' And the head cannot say to the feet, 'I don't need you!'" (1 Corinthians 12:14-21).

God has made you to be of service to His church. If you are AWOL, the body of Christ is incomplete.

Jesus has ordained the church as his instrument in the world and He has promised to return and gather all its members together with Him to spend eternity in heaven. The church referred to here is the universal body of believers who confess Jesus as their savior who, by his substitutionary death for us on the cross, is the payment to God the Father for all our sins.

The Universal Church and the Local Church

The moment you trusted Jesus for your salvation, you became a member of the universal body of Christ. You became a member of the family of God and a sibling with all other believers anywhere and everywhere in the world. As you honor the Lord in your business or career, you do so in kinship and to the benefit of believers everywhere.

While you are automatically a member of the universal body of Christ, you must be intentional in joining and participating in a local body of believers as modeled in the Book of Acts. The local church is the place to learn, worship, encourage, exhort, care for one another and employ your spiritual gifts.

In Chapter 3, we discussed accountability among peers and small groups. These small groups may be an outgrowth of the local church, but they are not a replacement for it. The local body of Christ is where God expects you to use and sharpen your gifts so you can also reach out to non believers more effectively.

A good church should challenge, refresh and motivate you to give God your best 24/7 at home or in the workplace. Corporate worship helps draw us closer to Him.

The Joy of Utilizing Spiritual Gifts

Note this chapter is entitled, "Involved in the Life of Your Church." That means more than just attending and giving. It means using the special gifts God has given you to put them to work for the Kingdom in the context of the local church. Many churches provide classes to help you inventory your spiritual gifts and then put them to work.

If you Google "spiritual gifts inventory" online you will find many free online questionnaires that will help you determine your best fit for work within the body of Christ.

You will be amazed at the joy you receive by using the special talents and passions God has given you within the church rather than just responding to a plea for service based on duty or obligation.

Recently, Margaret and I had dinner with some friends we had not seen in awhile. We formerly attended the same church and enjoyed the same Sunday school fellowship. The teaching in the Sunday school was awesome and the church was sound, but this couple never really found their niche.

They changed churches to one nearer their home and immediately were encouraged to plug into the area they enjoy most – helps. Almost every week one of them is fixing up a widow's home or working in a disadvantaged area. They have gotten behind the church's sponsorship of an African village and beam with joy as they show a picture of the little Ugandan girl they are helping. They are excited! Whereas before; they were just attending church.

When we lead mission trips, our main objectives during training are to lay the spiritual foundation of teamwork and sacrifice as well as identifying people's gifts. We will model the mission trip around the special gifts and talents that God has provided through the people He has called to be on the trip. It always works. People love to do what they love to do. God gets pleasure and glory as the gifts He has provided are maximized.

Margaret likes to tell how, as a women's ministry leader, she used to struggle in assigning tasks to the women for events like retreats and Christmas lunches. Also, she led a mentoring ministry for women where older women were matched with younger ones (Titus 2:2-5). She found it could be difficult making the right matches until she realized God already had brought together the people with the right passions and dispositions to get the job done. When she allowed God to work and the women to express their interests, everything just always fell into place and worked out great.

Assessing abilities and gifts is key to success of any endeavor, including business. My goal as a ministry leader is to assess our team's individual strengths and weaknesses. The goal is to maximize the strengths and minimize the weaknesses. I first learned this after my senior year in high school when I coached fourth graders at a YMCA summer football camp.

None of the kids knew anything about football and their skills were, to put it mildly, unrefined. However, by assessing their abilities and allowing their strengths to complement one another, we were able to put together a real team in two weeks. It was like the Super Bowl in the single game they played that climaxed the camp. They worked as a unit and won the game handily. This is when I first realized one of my greatest joys is equipping people to maximize their strengths and work together as a team.

Beat the 80/20 Rule

The final point is no matter what the impact of your business or vocation, it is not being fully utilized unless you are taking the skills and experiences God has provided you and are putting them to work in a local church to honor God.

It is a shame that the 80/20 rule (also known as Pareto's Principle) applies to church as well as elsewhere. In a nutshell, as applied to organizations, the principle basically states that 20 percent of the people do 80 percent of the work.

If we as godly business people and workers honor the Lord by putting our skills to work joyfully in the church we can do something about those numbers. After all, the body of Christ should set the pace, not follow the culture.

Chapter 14: Involved with the Life of Your Church

Discussion Questions

1. Discuss how all aspects of life benefit the body of Christ (work, hobbies, church, school, sports, community).

2. In what ways do each of us make up the bigger body of Christ? Give examples of specific spiritual practical gifts.

3. Discuss spiritual gifts and how to recognize the gifts different people possess.

4. Take a spiritual gifts inventory online and make a note of your gifts. Discuss them and how you are using them. A year or two later take an inventory again and see how the Lord is developing your gifts.

5. Does the church's role in our life encourage, challenge and motivate people to give God our best 24/7 wherever we are at work?

Personal Reflection

1. My spiritual gifts are _____.

2. I use my gifts in various ways. Think about it and contemplate how the Kingdom is impacted by how the Lord uses you uniquely.

3. The most rewarding experience I have had using my spiritual gifts is _____.

4. Do I allow God to lead me and work in my life?

5. Think about specific times where God has lead me to be involved in the life of another person and I have been obedient .

Chapter 15
Lovers of God and Neighbors

"Jesus replied:" 'Love the Lord your God with all your heart and with all your soul and with all your mind.' This is the first and greatest commandment. And the second is like it: 'Love your neighbor as yourself'" (Matthew 22:37-39).

This is the alpha and omega – the beginning and the end – of all the attributes of a godly person. Jesus continued in verse 40: "All the Law and the Prophets hang on these two commandments."

He also summarized all the Scripture in this way: "So in everything, do to others what you would have them do to you, for this sums up the Law and the Prophets" (Matthew 7:12).

Love is the root. Love for God which instills a love for our neighbor. Love which He pours upon us and through us. Love which we can gain only by spending time in His Word and in talking with Him daily about every aspect of our lives. Love which we demonstrate by our worship, fellowship with other believers and obedience to Him as expressed in His Word and as shown by our placing Him above all else.

All of this book is about loving God and others and showing it in the way we live and do business.

Don't you want to be friends and do business with people who treat you and love you as themselves? Don't you want someone who will do unto you as they would have you do unto them? God's spiritual command is also very practical. Enough said.

But nobody said this is easy. If you embark on being a godly business person or a light in your world for the Lord, you are a threat to Satan. Don't underestimate him. And don't overestimate him.

Now in the next chapter let's size him up, learn to recognize and avoid his traps and equip ourselves with the knowledge and power to defeat him.

Chapter 15: Lovers of God and Neighbors

Discussion Questions

1. Define love. Is it a command or an emotion based on what the Bible says?

2. Discuss ways of showing love for the Lord in our actions toward others.

3. How does our witness to family members show love of God? Give examples and share stories.

4. Evaluate how to honor God by loving family members and neighbors.

5. What impact does reading the Bible have on how you love others? Does it make a difference in "the condition of the heart?"

Personal Reflection

1. Do I really think about my love for God in everyday life?

2. How do I show it when I'm driving? At work? At home?

3. How can I show people love in a Biblical way at home, work and church? Think about specific actions that are genuine and not motivated by guilt.

4. Think about how God's command works in very practical ways. What are the positive results of God's plan?

5. Do I really think I'm up to the task? Am I sold out to follow Jesus in this way?

Chapter 16
Spiritual Warfare

When you purpose to do life and business God's way, you should visualize that you are drawing a line in the sand and taking the world. The battle is joined with the enemy of God, Satan. He does not mind you calling yourself a Christian and then living a worldly life. After all, the Bible says he is prince of the world.

However, when you stand strong for the Lord, you are a threat to Satan. He cannot snatch the salvation you received through faith in Jesus from you, but he can and will attempt to prevent you from encroaching on his turf and being a light to others in this life.

It still grieves me to think of the first group of potential businessmen The Rock trained in Africa. One evening while teaching (we always met outside) I took a stick and drew a line in the dirt. I explained as best I could that battle that lay ahead and asked who wanted to cross the line for Jesus. There was hesitation and some looks of fear. Then one stepped across. Then another and soon everyone took the step and there was great joy and unity.

Storming the Beaches

But, unfortunately, they really had no clue what they were getting into. One by one, the enemy ripped them to shreds as they tried to take their commitment to Jesus into the market place. It reminded me of the brave soldiers on D Day, the Allied Invasion of Europe launched on the shores of France, who debarked from the Higgins Boats that transferred them from the troop transport ships to the beaches. Many simply drowned when they jumped into the waters to storm the beaches. Others were cut to shreds by German gunners. For those brave men, their battle was finished early. But victory lay ahead.

The hard lesson learned from the men in this first group is that it is not possible to withstand the world and Satan for the Lord if your heart is not right. These men said and did what was necessary to qualify for loans through The Rock program. I am certain they even thought they believed all the concepts I have taught in this book.

It's All About the Heart

The difference was in this first group, I did not teach on the condition of their hearts. No matter what their mouths spoke about doing business God's way, the condition of their heart was to get their share of the funds from the loan program. I failed to teach them that the "heart is deceitful above all things" and they must give the Lord free reign to root out selfish and ungodly motives.

Also, we failed to screen the men as we now do. We simply announced from their church's pulpit we were launching a men's discipleship and business program with the potential for business loans. People showed up for the wrong reason – money instead of discipleship. Now we have strong pastors recommend men with a demonstrated record of accountability and potential for spiritual leadership and discipleship. We state up front that loans are not the focus of the program and most of those who attend the training won't get one. Now the men in the program tell us the Bible teaching, along with the discipleship and leadership training, are far more valuable than the loans ever could be.

The first group failed in faithfulness, accountability and openness. They exhibited a love of money. I remember the man the men elected chairman of the group strutting in front of them and saying playfully, "I'm a millionaire" after he received a loan for a grain mill. (He wasn't really a millionaire in the western frame of reference – a million Uganda shillings are equal to about $600 U.S.)

All of the men were influenced by non-believing family members and friends. Some spent their loan proceeds for things other than those included in their applications; others just dropped out of sight and did not make their loan payments. Some suffered true hardships – one was robbed at gunpoint and two others were the victims of theft. But rather than explaining their misfortunes, they hid in embarrassment.

Fish Tales

In the beginning with this first group, there was great hope and seeming promise. I recall two of the men, Moses and Richard, who were working together in a business smoking fish. They would purchase the skeletal portion of fish left over from fish factories along Lake Victoria in Uganda, smoke it, and transport it via a rented lorry to sell it at a market on the border between Uganda and the Democratic Republic of the Congo.

As newcomers to the market, they were derided by the competing veteran smoked fish sellers on their first visit. The competitors discouraged the buyers from doing business with the two newcomers. Richard and Moses then joined hands in the market and prayed the Lord would provide a buyer for their fish. Shortly afterward, a woman bought their entire load.

The next time the men went to market, a competitor threatened to hire a witch doctor to put a curse on their truck so it would explode. Moses stood tall and said, "You cannot touch us because we are saved men who stand on the Rock of Jesus!"

On a subsequent visit, the man who had threatened the two men confessed, "Your Jesus is more powerful than our witch doctor." All of this was told to the men in The Rock group and they were encouraged and enthusiastically clapped their hands.

But then the fish market turned south. Moses asked for additional funds for a deposit to do business with a new fish factory that was supplying fish cheaper than all the other plants. We loaned him the money but foolishly gave it to him to make the trip to pay the fish plant (now all payments go directly from The Rock to the vendor to avoid temptation of the borrower to misuse the funds). Moses decided without consulting with anyone from The Rock that he would go into the fresh fish business instead and buy a refrigerator with his most recent loan proceeds so he could keep fresh fish at his house and market it to restaurants.

So he bought the refrigerator, apparently not factoring in that the electric power in his area is highly unreliable and can be out for hours at a time. Predictably, the fish spoiled in his refrigerator while the power was down and he was out of business.

Unhappy to discover he had used his loan proceeds to buy a refrigerator without our knowledge, we instructed Moses to sell it and return the money to The Rock. He did sell the refrigerator, but used it to pay for his personal rent instead.

You can see how things can start strong for the Lord and then spiral out of control when difficulties come along. One bad decision leads to another and, when we put ourselves first instead of seeking counsel and the Lord's guidance, destruction follows.

Know Your Enemy

We cannot blame all of our sinful behavior, mistakes and misfortune on Satan. Some of it is just due to our own sinful nature and selfish desires. However, Satan is keenly aware of our shortcomings in these areas and will do whatever he can to exploit them.

Satan's goal is to distract you from God. As stated before, if you have trusted Jesus for your salvation, he can't take your soul. But he can take away your effectiveness for the Kingdom.

Simply put, there is one God and one enemy of God whose name is Satan. His plan is to get you to trust in anything other than God – whether that be your portfolio, possessions, intelligence, position, theology, philosophy, relationships or (in the case of Africa) witch doctor.

Personal pride is a favorite tool of Satan to turn us against God. After all, it was Satan's own pride that morphed him from an angel who was "the model of perfection, full of wisdom and perfect in beauty" (Ezekiel 28:11) in heaven to a rebel against God banished to the earth. He sought to put himself in the place of God.

"Your heart became proud on account of your beauty, and you corrupted your wisdom because of your splendor. So I threw you to the earth; I made a spectacle of you before kings." (Ezekiel 28:17)

Revelation tells us further: "And there was war in heaven. Michael and his angels fought against the dragon, and the dragon and his angels fought back. But he was not strong enough, and they lost their place in heaven. The great dragon was hurled down — that ancient serpent called the devil, or Satan, who leads the whole world astray. He was hurled to the earth, and his angels with him." (Revelation 12:7-9)

Jesus himself called Satan "prince of this world." (John 12:31, John 14:30, John 16:11) And the prince has an army – the angels who sided with him in the rebellion against God. These fallen angels are better known on earth as demons. These demons cannot possess or own believers in Jesus, but they can torment us.

As Jesus Followers, We Are Aliens

Because Satan is prince of the world, God clearly instructs us to be in the world, but not of the world.

"For though we live in the world, we do not wage war as the world does. The weapons we fight with are not the weapons of the world. On the contrary, they have divine power to demolish strongholds. We demolish arguments and every pretension that sets itself up against the knowledge of God, and we take captive every thought to make it obedient to Christ." (2 Corinthians 10:3-5)

We are told to consider ourselves aliens to the world. (1 Peter 2:11, Hebrews 11:13-16). Not only that, but we are instructed that "friendship with the world is hatred toward God." Hebrews 4:4 continues, "Anyone who chooses to become a friend of the world becomes an enemy of God."

So, as you can see, that line in the sand (or dirt) is clear. You have to choose. If you choose God's side, the battle is engaged.

Satan Attacks New Things

Beware that one of Satan's strategies is to defeat you before you really get started – either by tricking you that the world really is not a spiritual battleground or by knocking you down early just as the men in the first business group The Rock launched in Uganda. Satan attacks babies – new things. He tries to nip opposition in the bud before it becomes formidable and makes an impact for the Lord.

This was the case when God sent His son Jesus to the world. King Herod, terrified of the foretold Messiah who had come as a baby in Bethlehem, ordered all boys two years old and younger in Bethlehem and the surrounding vicinity to be killed. (Matthew 2:16-17) Though despicable and tragic, this incident shows the folly of confronting God and His son.

Expect opposition when you set out to do good or launch a new endeavor for the Kingdom. If you don't get opposition, you might examine why what you're doing is not a threat to the prince of the world.

Peter tells us that Satan stalks like a lion. "Be self-controlled and alert. Your enemy the devil prowls around like a roaring lion looking for someone to devour. Resist him, standing firm in the faith, because you know that your brothers throughout the world are undergoing the same kind of sufferings." (1 Peter 5:8-9)

God Equips Us for Battle

Praise God that He gives us all the tools we need to resist Satan and win the battle! At the name of Jesus, Satan is stopped in his tracks. "You, dear children, are from God and have overcome them, because the one who is in you is greater than the one who is in the world." (1 John 4:4)

We have been given our own armor and battle plan in Ephesians 6:10-18, which uses the Roman military garb as an example.

"Finally, be strong in the Lord and in his mighty power. Put on the full armor of God so that you can take your stand against the devil's schemes. For our struggle is not against flesh and blood, but against the rulers, against the authorities, against the powers of this dark world and against the spiritual forces of evil in the heavenly realms. Therefore put on the full armor of God, so that when the day of evil comes, you may be able to stand your ground, and after you have done everything, to stand. Stand firm then, with the belt of truth buckled around your waist, with the breastplate of righteousness in place, and with your feet fitted with the readiness that comes from the gospel of peace. In addition to all this, take up the shield of faith, with which you can extinguish all the flaming arrows of the evil one. Take the helmet of salvation and the sword of the Spirit, which is the word of God. And pray in the Spirit on all occasions with all kinds of prayers and requests. With this in mind, be alert and always keep on praying for all the saints."

The belt of truth is knowledge of the one true God; the breastplate of righteousness is Jesus and His blood on the cross which cleanses us from sin; the feet fitted with readiness is our ongoing love relationship with Jesus; the shield of faith is our unshakeable trust in the Lord; the helmet of salvation is our assurance of life with God forever in heaven; and the sword of the Spirit is God's Word as revealed in the Scriptures.

Often, we lose sight of the fact as stated in the Bible that our battle is "not against flesh and blood" but against "spiritual forces of evil in the heavenly realm." Before you allow yourself to get sucked into personal animosity with a business associate, friend or acquaintance, ask yourself, "Am I being manipulated by unseen forces of evil in the spiritual realm?" Remember that Satan wants to divide and conquer. Jesus desires peace.

When you are tempted to sin, recognize it for what it is -- a spiritual missile fired from the evil one. Call upon the Lord and He will shoot it down.

Note that the one offensive weapon mentioned in Ephesians is God's Word. This is the one and only weapon Jesus used when tempted by Satan in the wilderness.

"Then the devil left him, and angels came and attended him." Amazingly, you have the same power of the Word and the Holy Spirit at your disposal to fight your battles if you are alert and use them.

So suit up! God wants you to put on the armor and engage the battle. He will get the glory and you will be blessed for eternity as you fight the noble fight for His righteousness in business, home, community, nation and church.

Chapter 16: Spiritual Warfare

Discussion Questions

1. Evaluate the difference between outright sinful behavior and spiritual warfare?

2. Who is the enemy of God? How does this take different forms of idols in Bible history and in today's world?

3. Discuss specific examples of spiritual warfare. What were the circumstances in these examples of spiritual attack?

4. Give examples of how to recognize spiritual warfare and how to fight it.

5. What are some of the indicators of idols such as love of money and power?

Personal Reflection

1. In the last month think about times of discouragement, deception, depression and disunity? How did each incident begin?

2. After considering these things read Matthew 4. Think of the ways Satan tries to tempt Jesus in the area of physical, emotion and psychological ways. Does this help you see how to be alert?

3. Evaluate how the enemy tries to exploit weak areas of hunger, pride, insecurity, control and power.

4. Do parallels exist in my life today?

5. What will I do to recognize and protect myself from spiritual attack?

Chapter 17
Leading by Following

As believers in Jesus, we all are leaders whether we choose to recognize it or not. We are held to high standards and non believers crave to see us stumble so they can call us hypocrites and defame the name of the Lord.

So the question is not, "Am I a leader?" The question is, "What kind of leader am I?" The answer determines your impact for the Kingdom in your business, workplace, family, church and community.

As a Christian, I believe your first obligation in leading is to be a sold-out follower of Jesus.

With this in mind, I met in 2007 with two Rock scholarship students, Ben and Lutaaya in Uganda, who also oversee our discipleship/leadership training to university students. We wanted to come up with a creed which stated from the Scripture the heart of The Rock in developing leaders and disciples.

Too often in Africa and elsewhere, leaders serve themselves rather than those they are called to serve. Their egos dominate and their worlds revolve around themselves and others paying homage to them. In Africa, I call this the "big man" syndrome. We wanted a strong statement standing for Jesus' opposite model of serving rather than being served and humility over hubris.

The Rock Leadership Creed we developed over five days together has touched lives. One distinguished law student who is a Rock scholar has posted it over his bed and says he reads it every day when he arises and every night when he goes to bed. He says it has changed his life. Rock participants have taught the Rock Leadership Creed in churches and applied it in other organizations where they serve in leadership.

The Rock Leadership Creed is recited before every Rock meeting, whether it is with the Board of Directors in the U.S. or scholarship students and businessmen in Africa.

The Rock Leadership Creed

All: We commit to develop fully our God-given abilities to serve Him
and our country. We believe as leaders:
Leader: The best leader ...
All:... is a great follower of Jesus.
(1 Samuel 13:14)
Leader: A leader leads ...
All:... by example.
(1 Corinthians 4:16)
Leader: A leader does everything ...
All:... as if unto the Lord, not men.
(Ephesians 6:7)
Leader: A leader serves ...
All:... rather than being served.
(Matthew 20:28)
Leader: A leader considers others ...
All:... more important than self.
(Philippians 2:3-4)
Leader: Without Jesus ...
All:... we can do nothing.
(John 15:5)
Leader: With Jesus ...
All:... we are more than conquerors.
(Romans 8:37)
All: We stand on The Rock of Jesus.

Who would not want to follow a leader who lived by these Biblical truths? This is a radical creed in that it flies in the face of corporate strategies and worldly ways to get ahead. Anyone who puts this creed into practice will be set apart both in the eyes of the world and the eyes of God.

Mockers would say it is naive and a strategy for failure. In particular, many of the richest people in the world who are not Christ-followers might laugh at the statement that "Without Jesus, we can do nothing." From a worldly perspective, they are correct. The Bible acknowledges that on this earth, the wicked do prosper.

But that prosperity comes to nothing in the blink of an eye when our life is done. From God's perspective for eternity, it is absolutely true that we can do nothing of any eternal significance without Jesus as John 15:5-6 clearly states: "I am the vine; you are the branches. If a man remains in me and I in him, he will bear much fruit; apart from me you can do nothing. If anyone does not remain in me, he is like a branch that is thrown away and withers; such branches are picked up, thrown into the fire and burned."

There are many excellent books on leadership and my purpose here is not to add anything other than emphasis on serving God sacrificially as leaders, which I believe is the biblical model.

A leading Christian author on leadership is John Maxwell, who has created what he calls the 21 irrefutable laws of leadership. Not long ago, one of The Rock's university scholarship students requested we provide him with a Bible published with Maxwell's notes. I declined when my wife Margaret wanted to take him the book. Not because I think Maxwell's writings are suspect, but because I was concerned his emphasis could be taken to put the focus on self rather than others.

Interestingly, I later learned that Maxwell revised the book in 2008 after 10 years in print. He changed the book by asserting that leaders "add value by serving others" and that "people do what people see." In other words, there is now more emphasis on leaders' servanthood and the examples they set.[1]

---

1   Maxwell, John C. *The 21 Irrefutable Laws of Leadership, Revised and Updated 10th Anniversary Edition*, Nashville, TN, Thomas Nelson Publishing, 2008.

Chapter 17: Leading By Following

Discussion Questions

1. Discuss the "big man or lady syndrome."

2. What does it reveal about "the condition of the heart?"

3. Give practical examples of the Rock leadership creed at work, home, church or in your community.

4. Do you think about being "more than conquerors" in the spiritual realm?

5. Share examples where Jesus has rescued you in a situation where only he could solve a problem.

Personal Reflection

1. What kind of leader am I?

2. Do I exhibit good leadership characteristics?

3. Has leadership training helped me be a better spiritual leader and secular leader?

4. Think about the specifics and how leadership principles have been implemented.

5. Which character in the Bible do I connect with the most as a leader?

Epilogue

If you have made it this far in this book and choose to put into practice what you have learned, you will be entering through what Jesus calls the narrow gate.

"Enter through the narrow gate. For wide is the gate and broad is the road that leads to destruction, and many enter through it. But small is the gate and narrow the road that leads to life, and only a few find it." (Matthew 7:13)

Doing life and business God's way is a journey, not a destination. My life verse is John 3:30, "He must become greater; I must become less." Life on this earth is a constant surrendering of myself over to Jesus. Every day that passes we should be able to give Him more, and as we do, He enables us to give even more over to Him the next day.

I'm also partial to Matthew 6:33-34, "But seek first his kingdom and his righteousness, and all these things will be given to you as well. Therefore do not worry about tomorrow, for tomorrow will worry about itself. Each day has enough trouble of its own." I have given this verse my own personal translation: "Do the right thing and leave the rest to God."

To complete this book, I retreated to a friend's cabin in the Jemez Mountains of New Mexico near Valle Grande, a magnificent caldera near Los Alamos.

It was here in 2002 that I came during a major life transition to seek God's will for my life. I had held to my corporate job and resisted fulltime ministry. Then I was laid off from my job. God guided me beyond all expectations. Here is what I wrote in my journal on Wednesday, July 3, 2002:

"I lay in bed about 11 a.m. asking for a sign. Not a sign to confirm my faith…but a sign to give me direction. Ever since I arrived in New Mexico, I have been overwhelmed by the drought. Unspoken, yet in my spirit, I knew God was showing me this dryness was a picture of my soul. After I called the mission agency I decided to drive 15 miles to Valle

Grande for a bike ride. I'm excited about what God is leading me to, but hesitant to claim it.

"First I hear thunder. Now there are raindrops on the windshield. Could it be the sign I asked for? Is God breaking the drought of my soul? Is mission work in my future? Now I'm parked overlooking Valle Grande. I'm hesitant to claim this as a sign…it's more of a sprinkle than a shower. Then I decide to begin writing to see what happens. Lightning flashes in the valley before me. Thunder rumbles. Again lightning and again thunder. The sprinkle is now a shower. Lord, in faith, I claim your sign. Praise you, God. Praise you, Jesus. Amen.

"I see a large herd of elk…maybe 100 in the distance. Praise God its still raining. The air smells incredibly refreshing. Not good for bike riding, but I'm excited to put on my rain jacket and walk. Now it's pouring. Oh, water my soul, sweet Jesus! The space is open, refreshing and the panorama is not the same.

"II Samuel 22:20 'He brought me forth into a large place; he delivered me because he delighted in me.' Valle Grande is symbolic to this to me because it is such a "large place." I'm thinking of a favorite scripture of Audrey's, our daughter, which refers to "time of refreshing." Acts 3:19 I'll have to talk to her about it. Because it was raining, I removed my eye glasses for my walk along the edge of Valle Grande. How clearly I can see…both the panorama and every detail like pine needles, blades of grass, individual shimmering aspens and intricate flower blooms. It seems super natural and surrealistic. Yes, God is giving me eyes to see!

"I am aware this is a hugely important day in my life. Probably second only to the day I was saved. Uh-oh. Here comes Satan telling me I'm an idiot and this is all just an over-spiritualized coincidence. I rebuke him in the name of Jesus and shout praises to the Creator who spoke all into being.

" Here are more verses from II Samuel 22:29-36 which have been on my heart for years. Now they mean even more!

"You are my lamp O Lord, the Lord turns my darkness into light.

"With your help I can advance against a troop, with my God I can scale a wall.

"As for God, his way is perfect; the word of the Lord is flawless. He is a shield for all who take refuge in him.

"For who is God besides the Lord? And who is the Rock except our

God?

"It is God who arms me with strength and makes my way perfect.

"He makes my feet like the feet of a deer; he enables me to stand on the heights.

"He trains my hands for battle; my arms can bend a bow of bronze.

"You give me your shield of victory; you stoop down to make me great.

"You broaden the path beneath me so that my ankles do not turn.'"

God rarely reveals His plans for us in such personal and dramatic ways. But in His timing He does and will.

Is your soul parched? Is your spirit dry? Ask Him to refresh you. If your soul pants for Him (Psalm 42:1) He will not leave you thirsty.

"Blessed are those who hunger and thirst for righteousness, for they will be filled." (Matthew 5:6)

Give in to Him. Desire Him above everything else. Let loose of yourself and live only for Him.

Jump on. It's a wild ride… Never a dull moment… No regrets…Rich Toward God.

About The Author and The Rock Outreach, Inc.

Mark Noblin is president and co-founder of The Rock Outreach, Inc., a 501 (c)(3) non profit organization which focuses on African discipleship and leadership development through mercy homes, educational training, business development/incubation and mentoring.

Mark, who is married to Margaret, has one daughter and a son-in-law. He has been blessed with four grandchildren. Mark had a varied background in journalism, small business ownership, corporate sales and corporate sales management before becoming a full time missionary in 2002. Mark and his friend Dan Vick of Celina, Texas, formed The Rock in 2006.

The Rock Outreach is different because it breaks the cycle of African economic dependence by creating productive Christian leaders, disciples and role models who are spiritually and econmically free. The vision is to transform communities for Jesus in developing countries. The mission is equipping Christian disciples in developing countries to be faithful servant leaders in their homes, churches, careers, businesses and communities.

Rock participants are a family ranging from orphaned children to promising university students to budding and developing business persons. We encourage relationships between the age groups which produce lifelong discipleship and synergy as they develop their God-given abilities and practical life skills together.

The Rock needs ongoing human and financial resources. For information on how you can get involved in mercy homes, educational training, business/incubation and/or mentoring through volunteering, praying, giving financially and/or going with The Rock to Africa, please visit the website at www.rockoutreach. org.

Transformational Discipleship Cycle

Business Development/Incubation

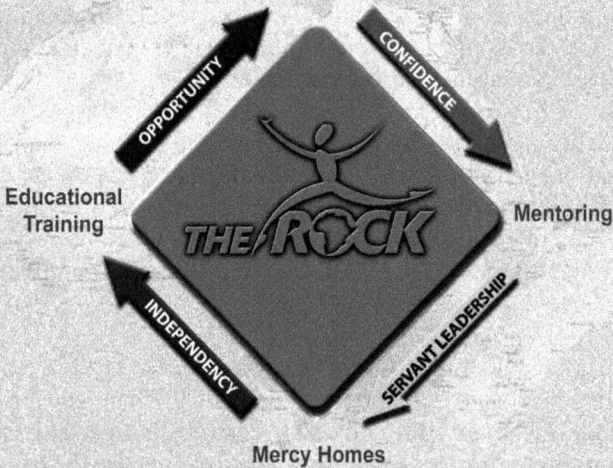

OPPORTUNITY

CONFIDENCE

THE ROCK

Educational
Training

Mentoring

INDEPENDENCY

SERVANT LEADERSHIP

Mercy Homes

OUTCOMES:
1. Self Sustaining
2. Community Leaders
   (Christ-Centered)
3. Biblical Centered Families
4. Fulfilling the Great
   Commission

THE ROCK
Real lives. Really changed.

The Rock Outreach, Inc., P.O. Box 670222 • Dallas, Texas 75367-0222 • 1.800.644.7453 • www.rockoutreach.org • info@rockoutreach.org

The Rock Outreach is registered in the State of Texas as a nonprofit corporation and approved by the Internal Revenue Service as a 501(c)(3) tax exempt organization.

Index

A

Abel 11, 12
Abimelech 28
Abraham 7, 18, 28
accountability 31, 32, 33, 35, 36, 40, 43, 100, 107
accountable 7, 31, 35, 36, 43
Adam 11, 59, 66, 67, 81
Adams, John 42
Africa 7, 23, 56, 61, 62, 69, 83, 88, 93, 94, 106, 109, 114, 121
Ahab 28
Aliens 109
Annanias 14
Attitude 87

B

balance 2, 70, 71, 74
Barna Group 21
believer 2, 21, 25, 26, 37, 55, 81
Bell, Rob 55
Bible xii, xiii, xiv, 1, 2, 6, 7, 9, 10, 11, 14, 28, 30, 34, 44, 48, 51,
    55, 56, 57, 60, 64, 66, 68, 72, 74, 87, 93, 94, 97, 105, 106,
    107, 111, 113, 115, 116, 117
blessing 5, 6, 8, 28, 62, 87, 96
Body of Christ xiii
business 1, 2, 3, 4, 6, 7, 12, 13, 15, 18, 19, 22, 23, 24, 25, 26, 30,
    31, 33, 35, 37, 40, 44, 45, 48, 49, 50, 53, 54, 56, 57, 60, 61,
    68, 72, 73, 75, 76, 77, 82, 83, 89, 91, 93, 99, 100, 101, 102,
    104, 106, 107, 108, 110, 111, 112, 114, 118, 121

C

Cain 11, 12
Chambers, Oswald 64
CHOGM 77
Christ xiii, 16, 31, 33, 37, 47, 55, 63, 65, 75, 77, 80, 84, 93, 99,
    100, 102, 103, 110, 115

N

Nathan 34
Nehemiah 54, 68, 69, 89, 91
Nixon, Richard 54

O

obedience 3, 5, 18, 20, 27, 35, 43, 49, 54, 74, 92, 98, 104
obey 2, 5, 7, 13, 33
obeying 2, 8, 13
Open 59, 65
Openness 61
overcome 16, 17, 18, 28, 35, 36, 55, 111
overcomer 17, 36

P

Pareto's Principle 102
perish 49
persecution 3
Peter 3, 14, 25, 28, 84, 110
Pharaoh 28, 44, 54
Philip 54
playbook xiii, xiv
poor 1, 18, 75, 83, 88, 89, 91, 92, 95, 96
pornography 17, 35, 38
possessions 1, 2, 6, 18, 76, 87, 88, 109
power 4, 6, 7, 17, 18, 33, 35, 45, 61, 71, 104, 108, 110, 111, 112, 113
pray 32, 33, 34, 35, 55, 59, 61, 62, 63, 71, 74, 83, 111
prayer 11, 13, 17, 32, 35, 36, 48, 57, 59, 61, 62, 63, 64, 65, 69, 94, 95
pride 4, 10, 18, 53, 58, 61, 109, 113
priorities 1, 2, 9, 19, 70, 91
prodigal son 84, 87
promises 26, 28, 37, 48, 49
Prophets 2, 104
prosper 1, 6, 61, 115
prospers 49
provide 5, 6, 10, 25, 31, 35, 53, 63, 68, 73, 80, 82, 83, 93, 94, 95, 100, 108, 116
Providers 80
purpose 1, 2, 27, 49, 72, 93, 106, 116

R

Rahab 28
Reagan, Ronald 42
rebuke 52, 119

V

W

Z

www.ingramcontent.com/pod-product-compliance
Lightning Source LLC
Chambersburg PA
CBHW060435090426
42733CB00011B/2280

* 9 7 8 0 6 1 5 2 6 9 2 1 4 *